CERTAIN

MAGICAL

ACTS

CERTAIN

MAGICAL

ACTS

□

ALICE NOTLEY

PENGUIN POETS

PENGUIN BOOKS

An imprint of Penguin Random House LLC
375 Hudson Street
New York, New York 10014
penguin.com

LIBRARY OF CONGRESS CATALOGING-IN-PUBLICATION DATA

Names: Notley, Alice, 1945– author.
Title: Certain magical acts / Alice Notley.
Description: New York, New York : Penguin Books, [2016] | Series: Penguin poets
Identifiers: LCCN 2016012657| ISBN 9780143108160 (paperback) | ISBN
9781101991879 (e ISBN)
Subjects: | BISAC: POETRY / American / General.
Classification: LCC PS3564.O79 A6 2016 | DDC 811/.54—dc23
LC record available at https://lccn.loc.gov/2016012657

Printed in the United States of America
1   3   5   7   9   10   8   6   4   2

Set in Bembo Std
Designed by Ginger Legato

ACKNOWLEDGMENTS

Some of these poems were first published in *Conduit, halfcircle, Versal, Interim, Maggy, Trickhouse, So to Speak, The American Reader, Animal Shelter, Vlak, Bomb, The Poetry Project Newsletter,* and *Strike.* The poem "Two of Swords" was first published as a broadside by Kavyayantra Press at Naropa University.

To Al DiPippo, who taught me Latin

CONTENTS

CERTAIN

MAGICAL

ACTS

o

"I COULDN'T SLEEP IN MY DREAM"

I couldn't sleep in my dream. The moon was a vast
flower but broken, behind leaves and the force
of distortion. Where does that come from? There's
no moon here. Distortion's all that I know. I walked
near the ocean unable to sleep. Trying
to receive messages, though I know there's no
one to send them.

Here are the words you were looking for. But
I wanted something different—Or is this it? Any-
thing, anything's different.

I left with another widow and a divorcee. I didn't
say goodbye. But that's just autobiographical,
who cares? I want to live here, where nothing coheres.
Who'd be in ordinary life, working or shopping,
looking forward to whatever it turns out it's about,
in the eyes of belief. I don't believe something. Here
I'm spooked, it's not that I like that, it's that
I stand in for that, rather. Though Here's so total.
Someone's screaming from the basement, who's going
away tomorrow; and I'm no particular age.
I have no fear. I'm only that I am this moment,
inside sheer unsteadiness, the night-time of crisis
as tone. Awake the banks are failing, but
I've nothing invested there. I'm listening for
something else, not Death, but what she hears.

She hears me, but I can't always hear me
saying to her, Keep me at arm's length. I don't
know a thing yet, and I haven't lived. I'm starting
to now, aren't I? No, you're asleep, you're
always asleep. I meet someone else who
knows nothing, the woman who said I am big-
hearted. I think about her but I'm dreaming
my dream. She flows into me then rolls away. I
approach my holy, haunted railroad stations,

underground networks, airports, trying to leave.
I don't know what I'm leaving or where I'm going.
I don't seem to mind, I'm in the state of
traveling. Suspended. That's always been my state.

This is my heart, or is it yours, I move within.
Death's faceless, looking for my face to wear
within her hair shape, just for a minute, before
she moves on to another. Everyone does it.
Well I'm gone. Not with death, but from
the market. Evaporated I've never been there.

I don't know how to dream but I'm dreaming.
In front of the house where I began; then I'm still
no one and everything. Everything circumscribed by
this child's body that's grown, but is
dimensionless near the dark tree. Enter
door once more—It's too *personal*. And
I go in, it's just a portal after all. I don't
know what's inside. Whatever happens next.
Nothing happens; things coalesce then melt
again, as if you yourself create them. Well
don't I? I create death, and time. Make
my story have a shape that's understood. No,

I won't be pressed for emotion now that I'm
back. If I hear people marching, mobilized,
I won't be one. I'm free in this house that
doesn't exist. And the crowd's passed
crying out for power. I have no needs.
No country, no continent, no hope. I sit in
blackness where I once lived. In magic, the only
force I recognize. What is it? a face
cries, skittering away. All that's left, I reply,
the basis of life, the explanation of
how I came to town. Oh, there's furniture,
some old couch I knew but can't remember,
tranquilizer of my thought. Press cheek to
it, sit on lino, breathe. I used to remember

this floor but I don't. I mean I'm just here.
I was cared for, and now I care for myself,
but I'm the early one too; though the carers
aren't here, perhaps the care is. Don't turn on
the radio, the old console, a period piece.
I'm not one. I'm immortal, like the universe.
All I feel is the tingle of this existence, or
non-existence, if you're an activist, handing
out parts out there where Death's invoked. Does
she come to them sooner, for all their rage to find her?

The sun is rising, and light enters my old
house. What sun is this? The desert star
or some one flame as in transcendence? I
won't ask it. I won't ask anyone anything.
I got tired of being childish. In your assigned
role you were a woman. But I've always been
a poet, that's all, no sex or race, no age or
face. Can Eternity strip me of it? That's only
another word. I'm inside myself, and inside it.
Today's the new fact. Are there others there?
Timeless, and loveless, this light touches me.
I won't need anything else.

TWO OF SWORDS

I'm blind with my arms crossed over my breasts, sword in each hand.
I seek justice in countervailing sharpnesses: you are in force
and *you* are in force. I can't help but be both of you. I wanted

to be able to take a side and will never again. These blades could slice
my skin, standing as they do for our fierceness, or should I say,
stupidity? If I drop both swords and rip off the blindfold, I still can't
leave, for I can't leave this world except internally. Who wants to
see us anyway? Two parties, or two sexes, two countries—armies—or
two religions, two debaters, two gladiators, two contenders for one
space. Is there such a thing as one space? Don't you want
to go with the winners? you ask. I want this noise within me to die down.

Democracy isn't efficient, and the only politics I recognize lies
between us, undefined, requiring no casting of votes. It asks that we
admit we're both present, all present, in the same multiform space—
within me or you. I would never ask that you follow me; I will never
acknowledge a leader. I am my president. But also, I am
everyone, trying to be with you, because I exist, and always have.

NINE AND TEN

Fearing loss of one consciousness in coming to another,
I woke up reanimated as a familiar agent of *some* state,
enjoying immunity from testifying about my previous
sufferings, since I wouldn't remember their particulars—
the 9 and 10 of swords. I live in this building. I am a caller
of souls, or words, for you never know what bit of spirit will
be magnetized where. One man is attracted to the letters
for *intention* but he can't read. I myself won't read this
after I've written it, any kind of past life pains me now,
treading unnecessarily on bacteria, misspeaking, being
discriminated against as a tragic stranger.

                          The devil card
has been disbanded since I can't remember to be tempted.
I'm told that I'm Wisdom, but how would I know?

You look incorrect to me, as if you are waiting for me to err.
A partisan left over from an election. What did you
think would be won?—you weren't running. Me, I try
to be careful. I don't let my thoughts plan on anything,
even their completion. I once tried to select some way to be.
It isn't a good price, that you pay for writing a poem.

I THINK FIERCELY

I think fiercely to tell you how I have mutated, O
shades; help me and speak too for you have changed, to be here
in a poetic space with my own spirit, we are our I.
Did I arrive in capacity before sea and earth
were formed, and didn't they make themselves, after a birth as
sweet chaos, maternal chaos, that I was formed across and

return to? Poet, someone says, you are surely our Poe,
for you are the maker of order, lights, crescendo,
and even a body to walk the stabilizing earth
saying the boundaries we love, not between countries, but
between sky, sea, and land, between species, between us.
Shouldn't we be separate in space, though we're together
in this space? Yes, I say, we must always re-create
our world, for chaos, encapsulated by us, must be
lightly reformed from. I love the uncreated but it
erases me, our I, and I could like that if I were that,
not I, but here I am!—distinct and adventurous,

ever changing. Once I was one with the air or sea. Once
I was a river that began flowing, says another voice,
or part of my wholeness. Once I was the first eyes to see
the diverse stars, lights ambitious in their beauty; I was
senses towards them. How could they, magnetic fires, exist without me?

In the golden age of my memory, I was fructiform
intellectually. I could learn anything, but what
was there already to learn? And one voice replies, How to
become, that is, change. As our land changes, hardens or dissolves
into sand across my larger face, my spine of mountains.
To become a person, you must be loved and humiliated;
threatened by those who adore you. I watched the first races
learn to fight each other: everywhere, wasn't I there?
I am trying to reach you, to subjugate you whom I love.

But when I began to differentiate myself from thee:
if I was ape and then no longer ape, or if I was a new

oceanic shape, curved fragile seahorse disjunct
from liquid per se, or if I was now anemone,
I was all of history in an instant, as a god
disguised as time. A shade's voice cries, I remember everything,
for don't I move with the authority of my forebears?
And what is infamy to me, if I am every species?
Did you murder another? Didn't everyone? he said.
And this blood on my hands is so local within the vast scheme.

Stranger you are asked to be parochial, to share our
customs and crimes. To speak as we do inflectedly or
not; to be small. Oh no! I cry, I won't be as small as you.

In the air, menacing it by breaking its tranquility,
I rage; having been vomited out from unity, consigned
to be hungry. But I speak—have I always spoken? The avial
numinous spirits of the nature I'm not thought to be of
communicate; I know that we species speak to each other,
primal translators between light and sound and thinking—
I ask birds what they know: I sing to discover the rude
unboundedness of space, and to unite myself with it.
And you, the other voices say to all, you chant and croon
and scream to us. Will we always speak to be together,
disordered capillary mane roars, and scarlet-black
dahlia shouts to pollinators with its color, Burn in my heart.

Vocality, protean, are you a song of cognition?
Is my body a system of lights and tissue connecting,
as I am bound to the authority of coalesced seriality?
I accede to the rule of my site, but I will not
let others govern me, though from my earliest memory
they enforce themselves; and I hide myself from thee. Will I
hide until I die? Do we remember, asks a voice, more
than we are taught we do? For our experience is conveyed
to us; but I remember looking down from the stars

at the sea. I remember being a wolf conjunct with powdered
snow, my white earth, and howling upwards to inquire of the lights
if they called their love to me, or if they would never invite

me to rise. Could I rise? But I had once been there. I remember
vigilance waiting for daybreak, so I could be a girl
again. Watchful I elude the shadows that have not found
their forms yet: they seem to cry out that they want to be gods
not humans. In those days we weren't always singular,
but rode the sea of consciousness like bubbles overlapped.
All I want is to be distinct, but oh who will I talk to?
In heaven gained, stuporous, will there be ravens, watching
to cry out? There will not be cursed lives, cursed shapes, impieties
of others' perceptions: there will be the songs of our one song,
and we will still be the voices, mind or minds, intertwined.

I WENT DOWN THERE

I went down there, played the drum, called to everyone.

I have found you because you're there, all of you.
I want to hear what you say; I'll speak what
you tell me to. I don't think this is about love;
you are telling me we need a new description.
Maybe a new language, but *you* want to understand it.
Everything I say from now on you are saying
to me. In many languages, from many faces; I'm your mouth.

I saw you
come to me
as if you were
a god; as if
a god were the
essence of all us.

I don't believe we can save our civilization;
I do, I do believe it.
I don't want this poem to be beautiful. I do.
I have no skills; I have no hope; I don't want
any hope. I simply want to sit here, in this
calm. I don't want the electricity to fail. I
don't want war to come here.
I DON'T WANT WAR TO COME HERE!
I sat beneath the tree for a while. There was only
one tree left. Here it is pouring rain. The two
men are in a contest to take over the world.
They will be voted for to make it seem as if this
is what we want. Don't ever speak to me from ecstasy,
my life is broken. Tell me what style you like though,

I need to scream: do you have that one? I want
a woman to be in office where I can see her.
The economy works like mythology, by changing the magic
in the story, like you change a person into a tree, a spider,
or a computer. The computer weaves faster than

Arachne, and outsourced casts a net of loss over us.
I see the net, it's silver, fine, it keeps me from resting;
it whispers in my ear with its superconductive
powers, you must go to work. I am sporadically employed.
I am by nature a peasant: don't you try to change me.
I want you to leave me alone. I am a middle-
class westerner, who deserves plenty and calm.
I am an Inuit, my world is melting. I'm an African immigrant,
trying to go home to Europe, return to security and peace,
which I remember from my human past and from longing.
I must see a woman hold power, significant power,
before I die. You won't see that. This is no style. None
of you are thinking to me in a style. I don't want to work
in this stupid office. Can we destroy the pyramids of power?
I mean, they're made out of dust. You're all just
dust and dried blood, you're dead. You are not absolute.
Why am I carrying a peony, in my mind? I am looking
at it, white with pink streaks, to present to the monument
of our exalted state. I killed a lot of people. I will always
have done that; when I die I will have done that; when
I'm dead I will remember that I have done that. I'm
not interested in style or syntax or vocabulary. But I am.

They crowd around me in the dark; it's hard to hear.

I'm crouching inside a dark space, near other
bodies, waiting to dock, hoping we'll make it across
this small expanse of water. Too many bodies. I
don't want him to take another wife . . . Do I
need him? Do I really have to have this life?
I'm screaming for food, I'm asking for grain.
There *has* to be enough for us, so give it to me, I
can cook anything; I can cook flour, or dirt.
I can cook locusts. I can eat grubs raw. I
can chew leaves, but the trees are dried up.
This is the story. The trickster is wearing a red
shirt. He walks across the space of the story. He
says if you make your mark on this piece of paper
and give me all your grain, I'll give you a house and

a television, I'll give you more stories than you've
ever imagined. Now I have no grain, no house,
no telly. The stories swarm in my head; the trickster
looks just like me, except he has a bushy tail
sticking out from his jeans. I have no words for
what I need. I think it is what we need; but do we
have to need something? Not very much. I'm
starting to see something, I'm starting to hear,
but I know I never really arrive. I wanted him to
love me, but then that wasn't enough. We
gave ourselves to each other, but then
we had done that. Which one of us was more? He
was always more. I am the desire you want
to have, so you can feel yourself continuously
inside the line of desiring unwinding against
the horizon leading to infinite nowhere.

Molting, the first rush of June is now September.
Prophesy if you dare. I can no longer find any
rationale for living. My life is as small as a firefly's.
I am always uncomfortable; often I suffer.
I go on wearing this tie, stiff as a hatchet,
around my neck. Tied to the tradition
of boss and cattle. I want more rice. I want
to see and know that rice is beautiful. I
don't want to speak this language that doesn't
know me. What can we do about our world?
Why do you all make me struggle? I have to put
up with these people who keep forming me. I can't
stop changing as they tell me what to do,
even though I resist them; I say I do but
I can't. Change will arrive suddenly for me.

Most of us are slaves, largely by consent. Or,
you could say we're brainwashed: women are.
I don't believe we have it so bad. I do, I work
in a shelter for battered women. I submitted to
a pharaonic circumcision. I, I have no
problems. I'm a distinguished professor in a country

that has always had a male president. I support
one of the current male candidates. I always wear
the clothes that I'm supposed to, for my status. I
have no food for my children. I'm well-off, my husband
beats me, he's a well-known inventor with several
patents. Who has changed as a consequence
of anything that they know? I'm sure I will change
before I die, unless I die today or tomorrow. Can't
we tear this building down, I mean, tear it down?
There are so many of us. I propose the founding
of a country like Israel for women. I propose
the following solution for Afghanistan:
airlift out all the women and children who wish it.
Convey them to that country, the new one.
Pull out the American and European troops and
leave the Afghan men there to battle for
whatever it is they want. But it isn't like that!
I want to move to the new country right now.
My child is dead, and I want to be with him
in my thoughts; I want to live with him in my mind.

The light took my face. That's all I want to think about.
I only want these moments between me and the
elements. If I couldn't see, I would still *see*, I know it.
I'm anxious, and my mouth is distorting: I need
to wear a hat to cover my hair. I have to
cover up a lot of parts of me. Everyone does. The
morning glories have already stopped opening.
I want to say something subtle, but I can't.
It's that, now that no one loves me, I don't mind.
I feel awkward, I don't know how to stand up
among others. Every morning I ask somebody
what day of the week it is, to make contact.
I'm signaling to others that I'm good. It's
now strange to live in this body. I don't
feel at one with it at all. I'm sure I haven't
always had this kind of body to be in:
where precisely am I inside it? I move my
toes, they're not so far away. I don't want

to talk to anyone, but I also have to say that.
I'm nervous about succeeding. I think
succeeding's a hoax. I think everything's a hoax.
I want to go back to where I once lived,
but it isn't there anymore; that one of me
isn't here. Are we now making a style?
I speak like a person in my language, with
the wind anxiously hovering, in a receptacle,
over my shoulder. I'm taking pills for my
anxiety. I get charms from a marabout. I'm
trying to make a girl fall in love with me; I'm
afraid it won't work, but it's a way of making
my love take an outer shape. I want to tell
you she wears scarlet lipstick, and her
shoulders slope down. The nape of her
neck is indented. She's very neat in appearance.

I'm roaring through your mouth, I only roar.
I am a wind of energy, I am evil, but
I can't stop and so I rush along, seeking
gratification. I won't stop. I don't want to. I'll hack
everyone to death that I can see. I've been
told to cut and kill with my blade. I will
do it and do it again; I will never apologize.
Why should I be sorry? I am not unnatural,
if I just am; and if the blood and smell are
everywhere, I must see and smell it again.
I have to keep knowing that this extremity
is mine. I know there are other things to do,
and we chose this. We had to. We just have to.
I was inside a house with a gangster with greasy
hair: I knew he was going to kill me. And so
I attacked him and fought him; I wanted to
kill him, kill him to get away. I had had to
strip for him, take off my red velvet dress,
but I had become too thin to strip for anyone.
I can't be this one who's just chattel; I
can't be this woman who's treated like an
animal naked in a picture for you, genitals

and a face of intelligence, but you can't see that.
You've been brought up to think it's normal
for women to be naked everywhere, and you
tell them to do this work for you. It's just
more work. A soldier's heart exploded, and I
was covered in his blood, it isn't an image:
the guy has no chest. Who am I here for,
for me? I am somewhere in this damned world
killing people for you, while you conduct an
executive session in a clean clear room with
light and glasses of water. That tie again, those
ties. YOU HAVE NO PRIVATE LIFE NOW!

No, I don't have a private life. Or is it
everything I think? I don't seem to want
anything others want. I don't even know if
I want something. To be perfectly quiet, still alive
with no one pressing me. Or keeping me from
eating. I have to have money for food and to
replace my appliances. I hate them. I don't want
community. I do. I don't like other people's fake
sentimentality; I don't like their politics, or
their religion. It smothers me. I, I need to feel
something with a group, I mean, I like that.
You can build intensity; you can do good. No
you can't; there is no good like that. And
nothing's for women except stupid things to
say like "She isn't feminine." I see men every-
where urging us to let them lead us once again
in this time of crisis. I want to walk away.
Leave the crisis. Throw out your stuff and
sit down somewhere; I've got a sandwich, have
a bite. I don't want to eat meat, it stinks,
it stinks like dead people on a battlefield.
I say the same things all the time because
there's repetition built into time to make it timeless.
I helped build it in, I help do everything. I
don't wish I were younger, I was more stupid then.
I have no interest in being myself, I just am.

I'm doing what I always do with this cornmeal.
I'm staring out the back window, the dahlias
are up like I like them, again. I can
walk out and be saturated with light for a
minute. I want everything to be bizarre; I
want not to recognize anyone. I want to
sing in a voice you don't own, that you've never
heard and judged. I don't want to know where it
comes from, even though it comes from me. I
don't want there to be anything to say about it.

I want to be
locked in this
situation where
he threatens me
then tells me
je t'aime.

I want to be in well-lit rooms with comfortable chairs,
but I wish I knew how to live. I'm walking in a forest;
I understand trees and plants. I don't understand
the harnessing of nature to light up a city with neon—
that makes me feel like I'm living in *your* dream. I
hate my dress. I want to know the thing
that will justify my time, all the time I've spent
doing shit jobs. Stupid work. I have a ladybug on
my palm. I don't move around very well now.
My life has slowed down, and I need to be cared for.
I give my sister back something for her care but
it isn't money. We are inside care, because we have
to be there—it's light and airy, though she gets anxious.
I want to tell everyone in the world what I know.
I didn't dream for weeks and then I saw the sun bleed
like a Seville orange. My history and civilization
are literally melting; everyone knows. Waiting,
so they can drill. I already have no point of view
except that of the fallen. I have no individuality,
because I'm a deadened thing. I want to risk my life
for my country. It's the only idea I can think of.

I've risked mine for my country all my life, being a poet
who is just a poet. I can't tell you a thing.

At any moment a force from nowhere could rip me
out of my life. I could die of traffic or weather,
I could die of war or my heart. I have seen several
people die. I have seen so many die that their spirits
now seem to cling to my back like flies buzzing
in my ear only; I carry them with me as I migrate.
I don't know where I'm going. I don't know which
country I'll die in. I don't know what the world will be
like when I die. What it will look like. What the air
will feel like. I now accept its collapse into an
ugly new nature. I saw a hawk in my back yard.
I saw a ladder-backed woodpecker two years ago.
I've seen a western bluebird, and a phainopepla.
It's like a revelation. I don't know how to stop
yelling at the people on the platform. No one
is kind to me; no one asks me what's wrong.
I'm looking at them because they're mean-faced.
My face is trying to get somewhere; I'm trying
to show you how smart and worthy I am.
I see in my mirror that my eyes are the same
color they've always been. They are for looking,
but you see them. I don't want to starve to death,
but I'm starving in order to stay in this country.
I'd rather die than be deported. Give me papers,
which are so fragile, and so abstract—why
can't I just live?

Why can't I
just live?

I think the new language must be the inclusion
of everyone. It isn't about technique, it's about
inclusion. I don't want to be included, but
I can't refrain from speaking. I know I sound
plaintive. I sound desperate. I sound happy,
even though the world is a frightful dream.

I am standing somewhere underground, in
an underworld, with all the others. I never
wanted this. I am one of many, but I am
unique. Saying "one of many" and saying
"unique" hurts me. I am just a record player now.
I am the dead. Or, I am a dead man. I
have never been words, but words have never
been words. In language I combine my flesh
with yours, and you with mine; my flesh
is tender, my skin aches from knowing you,
my hand can't really touch you, but if you
say "I" I'll say "I." I want to say "we" but I can't.
I can; but I think that I won't do that here.
I take a word like "morals" and try to weigh it
in my mind. It has no weight today. I think
it has, I just accept it. I don't ever want to leave.
I like to be here with the word "maintenant."
In this epoch I think that the Chinese are singing.
I think the Georgians are unhappy right now.
I think my own people are mixed up. I don't
want to be in love. I'm tired of another's thoughts.
I'm not, I can't stand my own. I wish you didn't
have to go through things I've been through.
I wish they wouldn't go to war again. I
don't think war is ever justified, it's only
about death. I am a warrior. I'm young and
strong, and I'm here to help you. I'm overwhelmed
by your reality. I thought you were words, or a thought.

When I go to say what I think, I don't want to
anymore. I don't feel like I am where you are;
I'm not in the world except by appearance. I don't
care if my words make your sense. I'm
communicating with blank. I want to say it in beauty,
or in ugliness. I like the beauty of being restored
to myself, in the pollen light, if it will stay
for us in the future. I don't know that it will.
I think we had to be so many once we made machines,
and I love us, but I've always loved the other species

too, the ones that are saying goodbye. I don't know
what to do. I'm always saying the same thing,
because it's so important. I'm not trying to define
us, and are we different from those we kill?
I didn't mean to kill a thing. I walk through
the program feeling blue; I hate the program today.
I don't want to call the electrician, he
always hits on me. I brought four children into
the world. Some people have fifteen. I hate
makeup. I like it. I think politics is money,
in the Maghreb, in France, and in the United
States. I had some money for a while, but I spent it
on my kids. I've always done my job by the seat of
my pants. Why am I alive? I think god wanted you
to live. I don't listen when someone says god. I don't
want to talk about god. I'm god, as much as it's
a word. I have a job that's outmoded, I care
about words. I don't care about them because you
already know what I mean. You read my mind.
I care because they're beautiful. I'm talented with them,
like a musician is with notes, but there's no system. It's magic.

I'm so crazy I can't know anyone anymore. I
listen to voices, see people who aren't tangible
to others; they sustain me, and I need them. Who's
to say who's really here? I'm calling to him
while I'm working, can't he hear my loving
thought? I know no other thing that means him but
flower, he is my flower. I hear voices in my
head continuously, at least one of them sounds like me.
I can't hear myself properly—recorded I sound different.
I can see my body from the neck down, but I can't
see my back, or my face. I am walking south.
I am going west. I breathe in allergies. My lips are
sealed, though I'm speaking. Everything I think's private.
I don't want the dead or telepaths to hear my mind.
I want her to love me. I am able to reach
someone by thinking towards them, partly in words.
I send forth my thoughts. I think a thought shape,

a flow and cloud, touch gold. I touch someone by thinking.
I have corneas and lenses on my thoughts. I have
stone grey eyes. I have brown-black eyes and
night-black skin with a purple-brown sheen.
I'm standing next to a pearl-skinned one with flax hair.
We're the extremes of our animal; we will never see
our own bodies, existing for the eyes of others. But I
have my thoughts. I love to touch quartz.
I place the azure next to the vermilion. I gasp at
colors that only our species knows, cochineal,
gold leaf, or saffron, lapis, green lake. Have I come
from another world to inhabit this body of mine?

I'm afraid the way I think is an anthropological relic.
I always reflect my tribe or tribes. I want
us to be better people. I scream, Don't touch me!
I painted my face white to mourn for them.
I couldn't stop thinking, my thoughts kept attacking
my head; I was my angry thoughts, but I also watched them.
I don't think you understand what a form is. It's
what exists and you're seeing it or reading it, listening:
try it on its own terms. I killed her because she had
been raped, I was supposed to. I'll never get
over it, I'm going to defend it forever. I want to
touch a phantom, it's the grey dove of truth,
Inca or Mourning. Or Scaled. White flies up
in my own breast: do you hear me? I need to
know the truth. I was once young and beautiful,
but that's of no interest to me. I was a handsome
man with glowing skin. I am so fragile
I can't speak. I have no food. Can you
hear me, all of you? I lost some fingers from
frostbite, I would get drunk and fall asleep
on the street. I'm dead I think and don't have
any more memories. I was tortured so I could become
a man. I think *normal* means whatever
the people say, but I'm not gonna say it. Is
it normal for me to starve? Maybe here in this
place that's always in drought. I was flooded out.

I'm waiting to be rescued by boat. For days
and nights I didn't know if I wanted to live;
my whole tribe was dead. So, I was the tribe,
I had to live. When I die, a wreath will be placed
on us. I must be more than my tribe. I see
that woman's back begging on our street. I think
she is Roma. I can't make my hair go into
a shape I like. I know so much, but do others?

I expect to hear voices forever, even after I'm dead.
Everyone was raping me there in that field, crows
or ravaging tatters all over my soul. I can
barely walk now; I don't even know who to
hate. I know what's happening, but I let others
direct me. I let others say what our laws and
institutions are. I want to be lawless; I want
to be alone. I'll pay taxes as a woman, if you
promise me equality, parity. If not, why
should I pay? I ran across the room to my
mother; I was bleeding from my forehead in a
thin stream. I love that color of green, as dark
as you can get. I want to be in a dark green place.
I caught tadpoles out there at that oasis and put
them in a jar, they have flat little heads. Every-
one's thinking something different I believe,
everyone's completely different. If you kill me in
war, you kill a unique person with memories
that light up inside me in fiery messages from
my past, my electric past. I hear a buzzing
wire in my head. I'm sickened by all the suffering
I'm aware of. If I can't speak for everyone,
who can I speak for, a category? I can't accept
an identity others give me; I won't be your person.
I rest all night in the eye of a hurricane. I have seen
so much as a human. Is there no one, nothing
outside us, to whom I can show what we know?
Is there no way I can go outside myself, if
outside myself is only more of us? I went
to a place like another planet where I felt good

without wanting something. I went to the top
of a mountain and sat down alone. I wonder who I
will know when I die, if anyone. Is death human?

You used to
take my breath
away. Now
no one does.

I don't want to bother anyone anymore, I try
to stay still. I have a fatal illness that will
eventually be painful. I don't believe I'll ever leave:
will I really leave? I think there's another mind
out there beyond us. I don't, I think it's in me.
I think the other's in me. If I find a you inside me,
will it be the human—the human potential—
or will it be the morning star? I am promising
to be good again. I am seeing the words I say.
When I leave to live in printed words, who am I?
I know I'm covered in old flesh and my hair is white.
I have so many ideas! I'm so full of thought
I can't remember what I look like. I will
walk safely and in peace from now on. If I can
have peace I won't need much else, if others
will allow me peace: isn't peace a human right?
To walk where I want without others minding?
I'm a woman and I can't go where I want
without being noticed. I want to be in my mind;
I want to move through this air like a slow bird.

Will I always be speaking here? I have something
important to say, but it's just that when I was
a child, I went somewhere and saw a kitten and felt
really good. I'm full of a lot of souls, but I remain
singular. I'm tired of my anger, do humans need
anger? They have to struggle against each
other. Do they? I have always wanted to be
outrageous, but outrageous seems to be large,
the biggest sculpture in the world. I would go in my

mind where the others wouldn't come, but then
they came. I let them in because they needed me.
I must need you, but why? I don't know. I
don't take anything for granted. I don't want to
believe, and I don't. I don't ever want to be corny.
I'm sentimental and I like it. I take a thought
and hold it close and pet it. I'm dying on this
parched field, I know that I will rise up and
fly. I can't remember my body from before
it was skinny. What will fly up is me and will not
look like anything. It won't have to eat.
I am looking forward to existence without
eating and without serving men. Go out and tell
women to vote for me, he says. I want
to vote for a tree, or a star, or a bear. I want to
tear this building down. I want to have
another cup of coffee. And then someone said
to me, Why are you so fierce? But I'm not that,
that's only in comparison, inside a framework of
our invention. Okay, I have to flee the storm again.
Or I could stay. I am being hounded for my
beliefs. I'm struggling to tell you, I'm always
in mothballs. I want to migrate, but there's nowhere
left to go. If I could only find an unclaimed space.
If I could only dream from the beginning! I have
love, and I'm afraid to die. I don't have love,
and I'm not afraid to die. I just want to sit here
forever with thoughts drifting through, trying not to
make my life finite. But I'm beating on a drum. For you.

WE THOUGHT WE WERE OUR OWN

We thought we were our own people for tens of thousands
of years. We thought there were others like us but who
identified with a different story: a truly other people;
but we are all the people aren't we, we the people? We
have forgotten how to be we the people, someone says.
Have we? says another. We, if we're the right we, are
the people. We can be we everyone, in the right thought.

We found our own true love when we were young, but we
didn't know why we had to do this. Hadn't we
always? And now, we don't know. Everything we
have done we can come to despise: dividing us into
the we of men and the we of women for example; and all
the other we the peoples we, the largest we, are composed of.
Can we truly be this most large we of all, all the people?
We are domestic and malicious, we are kind and empty,
we are purely stupid, sadistic, mortal, but if that, as
we replace us with ever more of us, we will never die.
I might like to die someday, someone says. I'm not sure
that I don't mind if we die. For I'm not sure what
living is, in that way that we always seem to be sure.
We who ever manipulate what we think, we kids.

We loved our mother and our father, for they watched us play
without interruption, across the long afternoon and into evening.
Then we lost each other to our new families, our most
desired we, we thought; why do we want now to find each
other again, the we of our beginning? Who do we trust the most,
as we cleave and uncleave and cleave again into successive
groups, small and large, in a time we define as us, our
history? Our time is only us. Time the substantial we,
epochal and great, as only we can see it, our particulars.
In the historical library, one reads our book. Don't
you want to know what's real? Don't you want to worship our
pitiless exclusion of the times we don't know, can't remember?

We found our shores walking across a shallow ocean
or rowing in boats. Or we just materialized alongside
the people we are most like who aren't people—maybe
they're people. Maybe the apes are people. And the birds,
lizards, and lilies, we say; fish and algae, the sweet other
mammals, the dear ones, the spiders and frogs. We the people,
who appeared before we were born, for some of us were always
there. We found us from before, but there was a long, raucous
before; and some of us are sad we can't remember it. We
have stories to complete, as in our long integrity, though
they aren't true. We aren't true, defining ourselves as
mammals with digits and brains attesting to our superiority
over other parts of our we, but there is no superiority
without our we, without all of us. Without us we are nothing.
Without delicate, exhalant flora we are nothing; without
mists, and stars and planets, and the creatures who live in our
bodies. We are all of us congealed into our definition of we.

We go where we live—there is nowhere else. We make
ourselves hats and gendered pants and skirts. We are sure
we are correct in our details; we are of our times, our
class, and our values, correct as only we know how;
and our machines excite us, so much that we consider
them us: we want them to think and act as us. We
are our body of the airplane, the computer, and the car.
We are our canon and our rebellion, but that is more
of the story we have invented that is urgent, appropriate,
and true. We are our songs and films. We are what some of us
say, that more of us choose. How could we love each other
without knowing how from our resemblant forms, our
echoing sounds? We can identify ourselves from our pastimes.
And our loves. For aren't we our loves, above all? We
hate the ones who are spontaneously different, as if
what they loved accused us of unhappiness. We divide
then; we don't know which of us are really our ethic or element.

We are changeable in our moods for we are what is. We watch
with our eyes of us the squirrel person streak across the road,
and with our hands of us we write words in a notebook

of our language. These marks as on an airplane wing blazing
are words for us to read, though some part of us can't read;
some part of us is unlettered and describes us by living.
Some part of us has no leader, no police, and no protocol.
We in that part are above us, are the us to which we'll return. We
knowing the clear-edged poem of the object we see as us,
we who act. We could never sit at this kitchen table
without our terrible and beautiful past and our poems that tell us
who we are. We know ourselves inside the extinguishable
light, but we know ourselves in another universe: we
are here by our agency, which we cannot remember. A
world like a boat passing by, and perhaps another on the dark
water. How could we stop being us, even when we leave
the jeweled cinema? We are gravely and lightfully blessed,
but we bless ourselves. We are our way, but we fight
within it and about it. We step on the fragile thread of our way,
going about with no other explanation but givenness: this
is our gift, but who or what can have given it to us except for us?

VOICES

·

I am always the spirit of more than myself—
See the shade of more cling to me as shade, if I'm an image
if a soul is.
          I secured this new country
with my blood; I'm violent for the good, or was. I came from
an oppressed lineage—and did I once allow oppression, until
it came time to kill? For, so far, you must kill. You, too, will—
it says to me. This was a real soul speaking; from
the mother tongue; and I too am oppressed. I can't kill with weapons,
but I believe I can kill. I am coming to believe
in a soul's violence; or else, he'd extinguish my will, my
ability or skill, to be suppressed for further millennia:
it can never be you. But the national soul cries, *I am* the city.

I am taking the city for my own, I who am more
than one. I will construct a new soul violence, and so, will heal.

There's no one I can be wrong to. No judge. Who knows? Scarlet cloth
with surly dark shadow. Ancient language gets blown all over me.
Stand right there, in my mind. I could put on a lapis robe
and become Queen of Hell, and no one would know. Or Heaven.

Bite into this concord grape. Eat nothing else until I say to.
Purple flavor begins within. Stroke this stiff gold cloth—it's yours.

I want more. What do you want? I don't know any more.
It's different at different moments: it isn't love. Sometimes it's sway,
a dominion over the moment: I want it to be mine, in beauty;
I want it to be in and out of me like a light. What's a light? A clear

gold thing. I want to concentrate all my power here. I want all others
interested in power to stay away: they can watch, but they can't interfere.
I am the owner of this moment, but I'm not here as that, though it's
mine. The marks love me, the words love me, though I didn't ask.

There is an orange globe—not an orange—appended from a sketchy tree.
I have just transcended my epoch; I am alive outside written memory.

I or we. I'm standing before you dark ones in the dark, shadows,
souls. Do we know we're here and always were? Outside of combat;
outside class, thin ability, obese presumption. Outside
everything we think we are, cultures of progressive men
with women on their backs. Civilizations of people who wear clothes.
Everything we are in unreal day forcing each other through mazes.

I can't see a thing in here. I think we are remembering
and I'm your instrument: simply a sound, no nostalgia. Adult.
Let's hear it for us. I mean that. We are the music we hear,
abstract with abstract tears, asking me for an interpretation.
You entered this hall in your moonlit unconsciousness pleading
for a different life. You're here without knowing it; therefore
attentive. Where did we really come from, the horizon, or nowhere?
We come from sleep, where we are now. We come from the district
of tissue: from details that obliterate design like seafoam. Forget them.

One thing I know is that I'm full of blood. Who is speaking?
Blood confirms my identity; somebody else owns me, whom
I fight for against others of the same vulnerability, sack of migrating
ability. A drop of me was first spilled, my surface of jingles broken,

my surface invaded by archaic tooth of the enemy god's representative—
No, before that. I fight because I might as well, look at the barbaric
assholes calling themselves government: they mean *power*. I'd
rather just kill. Join the ghost dancers later at the ossified bridge to trip

over crushed skulls across the river whose origin's emotion—fake
panaceas of warbling values, religious nuttiness, con art—to partake,
finally, of livid equality, death. As I say, for I get to say, blood

has kept me going since it first turned red, or before. I am my own
shrine to the sanctity of the liquid—gluey, smelly, gleaming
as it flows behind the arras of political complexity: the leader

isn't the fated one, he's just a party hack. I'm fated, and I'm entirely yours.

You who are interested in my false memories of Troy, beware of me.
I don't mean Troy, I mean, oh Atlantis or Lutèce. Lavinia. Some
city whose name will come to me—Pacifica. Cracked Head. My
head was cracked in the pacification of Pacifica. That's why I don't
remember; this compensatory story comes to me like a dream or life,
woods of detail for my real but unanchored, magical
consciousness. You who are interested in the original tale, of our era or lot:

I sleep in the lobby of an ancient hotel. In the middle of everyone.
I have to have a husband; I'm pouting since he's got the menu
and won't tell me what we can eat here: chickpeas and millet, mesclun.
Why can't I just know? In this dream of my voice that's uneasy,
We can stabilize it, he says, for I have conquered you. I am your
president: all others rejoice, where are your lilies to strew for me? I

leave him in the compensatory night: what's real is who I am, the *exists*—
Is a woman back, to genuflect to an opal? The walls are bugged.
Button up the roaches, so they stay behind the spatial escrow

of those refusing their freedom. They stare. Everyone you know, totem pole.

The peacocks in the yard are all of the blue-green variety;
I got them to help us in the night. A sad tiny mouth top of the street
should turn into peacock achievement! I want to be a star blown in
the wind from the river, one of a thousand empty things on its breath. What's left

of a sister life could be display, iridescence, wham! Not your idea
of an old building on a rundown street—I wanna be a peacock!
So I bought some, at least in this dream or daydream of mysterious
brain with barge broken viaduct thoughts in the giant gold war
of washed-out civilizations. I *am* a habitué of my own thoughts

but I don't know where they come from, and that's pleasantly scary.
Buy yourself twenty or thirty peacocks, they'll shit all over the grass,
I thought, but it's worth it. When I was a kid I wanted a peacock
feather, just a feather. I must be trying to be some god of mankind,
I mean not your average destiny moth banging around in the dark,
but something like a king! An eternity of angel clothes but better.

Why am I showing you this piece of wishing? Because we're all poor,
and this is a rich dream—I don't care about anything else, I want to see
peacocks in my back yard right now. Then I am them. And they are better
than toppled sorrow, or Chinese music box, or red-flowering weeds.
I like to be peacocks. I hate the blues; I hate being worse off than someone else.

I spied on silly boys. Men, I mean *them*. Then, joined up with that crew.
I must mean, we were spies, we poets were. Is that a metaphor?
Do they know anything? Now, I know, No. Or, maybe just a bit
that I once didn't know. Back to the spies. Met near the older park.
My friends, my older friends; yet I learned something from their
scared and distantly held, good will towards me. We the embroiled poets;

I mean spies, including Russians like him, General Something Breath.
I meet him accidentally in the park. We see another of us,
Or is that one truly a spy? He's one of us? I don't know, let's kiss so

he can't see, legibly, our faces. Isn't he named T.U.?

The general and I kiss intensely. We've forgotten T.U.
is it *tu*? Can there really be a *tu*, or *et tu*? Poets don't know. I don't.
In this space, what do I know, the general? Am I now spying for
poetry, or myself? It was ever ours, ones in the space of words—

I spied to be here where we are, all in unknowing. And I loved
this General, can't remember his face; I fell for him. Was him?

It's me, isn't that right? I'm what I knew. Acts came from me—this me?
I did not do those things; I only watched, watched myself act, react.
Emotion isn't really what I felt. Reasoning was quaintly
of use like a superficial tool. Living, one is so detached.

Stupid carrots were served at our table in the night of signs.
I don't care about them now. I won't eat the orange reflexes.

It's me, not about smart. Me not buying up, not trying, former
banker or hustler. No-origin me, in the white-blossom night
I'm the secret, spreading and moonlit; I don't dance in code anymore.

Yes I wrote on our walls, calling our fate. Can't I abandon it?
how I'm ordinary, love you by resemblance; what's criminal?
What does it mean to me? I was in paradigm of subtle force
a swindler, but that's words. I use them here, without my trappings:
money, versus your trappings: morality, overlaying your
urge to make wealth using me. I swindled you. Like you, I'm

contemptuous. Enormity of our cons, carrots, who cares?

Merging with others my fate, am I not you in the dark?
We hear each other's voices, see her speaking for us, shadow
on a page or onstage, when one acts with the figures there; identi-
fication and the actors are us, right? We're the same, I'm you.

Primitively I saw greatness in the form of a great one, his rise—
did I really need to, who, I? He slipped on the ice thaw of his throne,
positions slid, the pole melted. I still served, in the night of demise,
but if the planet collapses . . . I mean, in our failure, should one serve?

No longer the dream we were invited to long ago, to watch
the great perform for us, legislating all of our love, wearing
our best clothes and gems; brilliant cars driving them to Descartes'
house, pretense they're better there too, in their fat brains.

I have to change, I have to kill them, I have to find my origin;
arises the Calling Star of us: save us, pull the play down.

I don't understand what I wish. It's thwarted whenever I come here—
I think I want to be his pretty sweetheart: but he's a frozen dark face
here, he's another, a mask, and I sing You're so sexy, as he leaves
to wage war against unsociable thugs, enemy blossoms in the hallway . . .
no I mean, I'm just a sucker, but you are incomplete unattached to me . . .
He's going to kill mystery enemy. I, I suddenly know I have to

bring down the Hôtel Terminus, who is it, I see it's him, the Falling
Tower. You're so sexy. If I die and there's no sex in the subsequent
night, pursuant victory of the Justice card. Just that, justice. I go after
on stairs of shadows beige and blunt. The guys called me cunt. Yes I'll

now devour you with bullets, with weaponed doom. I'll kill *you* . . .
notions of morals masking indulgent sadists. I can't love you.
Why are you like this? Why did you hate me and make me hate you?
Why did you think you were better than I was for thousands of years?

Yes I'm sorry and I'm free. It was not metabolically
possible for me to live; I looked at people replete
with constructed circumstance I couldn't believe in,
their parallel acceptance of an, at best, flickery
narrative. Ill, as they said, or melancholic

I, a kind of stressed dove, ever mournful of being born here,
star of my own supreme insight and mouth of decoded hoax,
eye of our thin model of alive—what is that—took myself
out of our world, wanting no more slender texture of yellow
air, puling words like hopeful, lonely: what could they be to me?

Now, I feel nothing—what I always wished when I was alive.
I didn't want evolution's wiles coursing through my blood—
Why should we have had feelings, anything so clamorous or
hurting? Or allusive to false reasons one took seriously:

It was not a serious world.

You talk to me in your sleep, the only time you talk to me.
You call me indigent or some such shit. I'm a watcher of doves,
that's my profession I invented myself, observing the doves here,
in our province or providence, where I'm allowed because I allow my-
self to sit beneath trees in the park, quiet; thinking of the other
jobs I too have: inspector of a tangerine, archduke of space around me,
theoretician of rustling paper bag life, elder watchman of light,
that the sun come up again. Fanciful, useless, etc. Your jobs shit behind a bush.
Your jobs create a miserable planet of bad air, stress, and warfare.
Even when you teach you teach how to get ahead: there is no ahead.
And there's less of it—of no ahead—than there once was. You think you support me—
coins, even government checks: I support you, making sure the world's observed
for what it is, so it can go on. I can't do it alone much longer.
I'm beginning to hate you, and that's bad for me. I had to stop drinking,
I'd become too angry. When I slept I was indignant, I didn't em-

brace the universe's motions so it could keep moving within its own self.
You think that's mechanical? Assholes! You've killed the common will to love,
changed us into a disagreeable space of steel intention, meanness—
I keep it all going muttering in the night's pumps; the doves themselves moan
in their sleep, they cover me, dreaming they can't fly and their throats are stopped up.

I defended another land, country I happened to know—
wasn't it an accident of fate that I wasn't from there?
Where should I live? What difference, momentarily to be
parenthetical in a flat or to be lost in language
fortress inescapable, other world of eyes against you.
Does it have to be like that, babe? I am applauded at night
in a bright full-up theater, for an act of bravery
in a country not of my birth, but where was I truly born?
I can't remember what I did to deserve this acclaim. He's
using the passé simple to describe how I fought for la France . . .
I haven't done a thing, all dissolves, my countries are pink birds
flying away. What country do I come from when I'm deceased?
Will we be together, all cultures together, erased? I
think we'll talk but without our tongues. Scrawls of essence.

It's grey, misty in here, silver like winter in a city park;
nothing blooms, but it's implied by the fog. Isn't fog fertile?
You don't know what will be there when it lifts. Blackbirds sing anyway,
start in December, somewhere up in those trees supposedly dead—

I'm going to name it, this silver-grey area, Grace's Park.
When I enter Grace's Park I'm not sure where I am, what I'll do—
say? There is a happiness from nowhere, has no reason,
made by nothing, for no purpose at all. It must be what there is.
There may not be anything else except gross dramatic action.

Outside Grace's Park are brasseries with neon signs, apartments, cars—
indications of the story so far. One's body has one too,
a story so far—we wear it like it matters but is unmarvelous.
Now in Grace's Park *it's* misty, *I'm* clear. If I'm as silver

as color I'm a phenomenon, silly I'm not that. I'm true,
truer than any name. These words mean something exactly when I
say them. In Grace's Park I'm free to speak. I was expected here.

Fleeing through forest turning silver, in the primal moonlight
smeared on us we ran like horses, only when I dreamed of him
in the literal time when he, he who only came to me dreaming,
as I dreamed—was he there? We fled you others, corrupt
compatriots, love without a bed, in the woods its dark arms.
All of it illusion of ice, broken behind us running.
There is nothing but unbroken ice all over us til we run—
til we have escaped from the world; leave it and leave all thoughts—
they weren't mine; now I can think, alongside my own lover,
this is the first time that my brain has ever sung on its own;
he will die because it's a song; you voices made it up—No,
you assure me, didn't he die fated to suffer reverse
in the architectonics of, someone still owns it, poetry?
My daimon survives as a ghost, telling me to tell it to whom-
ever, it is you, voices here, room of the shining sounds.

One bomb grazes a house, or is it long ago, out of the
memory I can't have, where does this imagery come from,
marginal static? I've never seen a theatrics of war except
movies, they don't communicate the fear, please don't happen
like children who never say anything after, though I won't be mute.
You don't need bombs to kill people, swords can be effective,

stones, arrows everyone screaming on both sides. Survivors
remember like me who never saw it. Archetype theater replays
in here so you run or fight don't think, that's what instinct must be,
I'm slowing down to reflect not opine. Offer up candles in peace,
to whom? To river winds, to the border gods who carry you to
sanity, the only place I want to see for centuries to come,
always alive in the collective sense, I who call myself Joy
fleeing in order to speak again, let me tell you I'm still alive.

I'm empty in the cold, cold in the sense we're not emotional,
speak, listen in the dark like some classical underworld but not
where we're dead, no one dies: place proof of that. *I want to reach your voice.*
It's what you were to me, liquid, meandering. Love's object.

I cried in the kitchen, his death was stupid at such a young age.
Then I hear him in my head, commanding that I not cry for him.
Why not? I ask. He says, There are so many others to cry for,
and besides we're happy. You're happy? Yes, he says, yes we are.
I cried again. He repeated, Please don't cry for me. Firmly.
He's only in his twenties but he knows what he's talking about,

if he's dead. I'm not going to think he's unhappy anymore.
I'm going to be cold. Each word beautiful ice that can melt and
refreeze, look at these diamonds in the no light of the mind of us.
Nothing can be explained; voices are what count. I heard him again.

　　　If there are always two ways
to exist in time, as I've seen, one is denser, the other's told.
　　　I'm always drawn to thick time
presenting fibers of chaos, bundled but indicating
　　　wildnesses as really grouped.

If you don't understand me, then it must be experienced.
　　　She was a dark-eyed woman
set like an emblem in the room replete with reality—
　　　how did I know the room's name:
real time? There's no time until you count: aging's not time, it happens—
　　　call it a beauty. I stayed
in the thick-aired room until war came ending the economic
　　　slump others read as story:
it was smeared in elegiac details on the brunette's young face.
　　　That's how I know it happened.
I'm alone as usual impossibly nowhere or right here.
　　　I walked a path, formerly.
Now I see things all at once, so this room's sufficient, painful
　　　because of visual courage.
Time exists to be brutal in. War is the beloved, undoing
　　　story—institutions—
bodies in time, on chaos' side, but I know chaos just sitting.

Is there a chorus of us? of a night, in voices thinking in unison,
a group to counteract the lonely mind? Hear how my voice multiplies.
I am a chorus, a group: wanting to be an us and so not guilty,
for we can say what's moot or seemly, what should be canceled or killed—
killing together's not wrong, nothing's wrong, until we, chorally, say so.

The dark dish filled with heavy blood is ours: but it's set in front of me,
I'm coughing diamonds of novelistic scenes en face, in a life outside action;
we killed some children, no we killed them together, you watching killed,
watched it onscreen I mean; doesn't want to betray her by having a drink
with me. We fall apart into these individual entities,
so I know I was responsible, or was I defending something—us,
a billion of us with land and time, too many for an own remorse—
regret and guilt are over; walking densely through streets hanging on to self,
I've tried to be a horde but I'm a blank star, billions of those on fire.

I have to get the keys to Rusty in a bar in Phoenix this night.
And no one else cares if I drive across the state in infrared light.
Just because it's a desert like the Gobi or any Chinese highlights
that I'll try not to get in my eyes as I near what matters to them.
In between grief so flat like you'd desire it, hardly any characters.
Didn't want anyone to find me, not yet. Billions hide me before
I can arise on my golden wings or something; Rusty wants to happen.
Don't you dig that as I chatter in anger with photographers onstage?
It was becoming too unworldly. Hold still now so we'll call you something.
Maybe the People's Republic, too passé, no? Bite this kumquat and live.
Starving in winter with tears in my eyes. Why did I get human features?
I don't know what the hell I'm doing, feet with toes? I don't know how to think.
And I don't want to think. Destroy my DNA or whatever it is—
civilizations and species recognition: vanity. Oh it's Rusty,
I've got your keys so you can go home now and translate your poetry
into the language of angels in bark clothes or darkest maroon at dusk.

     This is a voice in our head
meaning that stage we're projecting before our intellectual
     eyes, where we meet, unify:
Death is beautiful the way you are—is what the dead man says—
     voice of a blue gentleness
as the room's abstract and twilit. I'm the calm mouth of his voice.
     Death is beautiful, the way
you are—I take that to mean, one is. If it's so beautiful
     why must I live now, live first?
It isn't *first*, now isn't first. You must know that you're always dead . . .
     And if I am I must still
bring down the pyramid, the paradigm, the leader's pearl throne.
     Isn't he wonderful! scream
the children outside on pallid streets. Shining beautiful, like death?
     Death is now of another kind,
death in idiotic worship. Not beautiful like I am
     but a moral consigning

of all worth to one more man. Who is smarter than I am,
        if I am as beautiful,
as paradisiacal death is? I'm of the dead so I can't wait
        until I die, to kill what
deprives me of my liberty. Humans don't need leaders.

        Three thousand years ago, I—
what I always say, in what language? Akkadian I think,
        now I'm pushed out as new sounds—
How do I understand what I'm saying in your mouth bravely?
        eons of the chains of human
relationships ago (ended, futilely severed, crashed)
        I sold a product, myself,
not a temple whore but a simple, pleasant woman married.
        I was so admirable,
bracelets, the female values; fashions of our quarters,
        merchant class you'd call it now?
Climate collapsed while I was living, you would say—how do I
        know what you'd say? The dead know
all your psalteries and platitudes, I was so stupid I grieve
        for my lack then or at the
wind, the hot holocaust effacing millet fields and lifting
        scorpions to dominion:
I was always graceful and cheerful, empty-minded, as one now
        perfects servility—
everyone wants to serve the one who knows everything.
        "Knows" doesn't mean "knows," it means
"rules"; nothing but overreach and indoctrination of "knowledge":
        what do you know? do you think?
Wander with me among migrating useless ideas
        bewildering marks on air
unnecessary as my looks, my disposition, changed, crumbling sky.

When my brain chimes I'll know I'm in the answer.
Honor to whisper to bosses placed within a jelly glass
on the hundredth shelf above patchy linoleum.
I still accept you like weather . . . *I don't want to work for anyone.*

The future keeps backfiring. I can see my soul
entangled in others' schemes for how I serve, elaborating
the consequences of their echoed prerogative—
Redeeming your call to hire, as if you had the only right
to say how I should live: within a pay structure
not within the real: I don't want to work for anyone.
I'll be content when glue peels off the cardboard walls,
when the skeleton of the main house collapses and stains us dark

with chaos, I'll escape, at last, alone and dry,
not winded though, a mouth with teeth, a page, a scream or frail song
but no employee of lost vacuities,
gestures no one recalls the origins of, period-piece capital.

Breaking like mica to pieces of opaqueness—only for outsiders—
we were the new city states, supposedly a dark ages occurring:
only the big states are valuable, valorous—led by heroes, more like
portholes, empty windows on oceans of fright. In our city we forgot
about leadership, busy ensuring that electrical current flowed.

Federal government had collapsed, because computers fell when
scorched again the capitol couldn't mend—we unwound in chaos:
war, weather, famine, a traditional mixture—in our city I changed.
None of our concepts of social order, conventions of male and female
had significance—many men had been killed, women formed the council
responsible for decisions. I think I am a voice from the future.

I searched for you, or for him, or for one, every night as I lay sleeping.
Outside the walls of the city I walk: I can't require the old climate.

Form is what we make of it, changing it. I command it to change
once again, reconfiguring us from itself so we'll have love nonetheless.

Justice lies within any one of us, all of us together,
certainly inside me. Justice isn't only for men, owning
it by all appearances: aren't they the majority of judges?
I decide to judge by myself; the rational parts of others,
obeisant to judges' power are unjust to me. I pronounce you
all, unjust. What can I do, practically? Oh you want to kiss me.
Centuries ago, before I became a mineralized statue,
I resolved to starve you of me. You didn't die, of course, others
loved you, fetishists of power relationships. Now, still frozen,
but to call myself Vengeance I find I can move slowly,
then, having no control, I become a weapon, only form I show:
no one's seen it before; apparently light, a heap of dream,
rayed imageless energies, golden but toxic. I am now
a killer and am immortal, inorganic, an intellectual stranger.
You can't control me: I'll destroy you, a Nemesis, with my mind.

How can we disattach ourselves from those binding us to their use?
How can we destroy their power without losing *my* own will,
my precious sovereignty? We cannot have leadership—I will act.
I am a crystal skull, finding yours in order to plot sedition,

reading your messages: I have a substance, a chemical to
inform our broadsides, change dream's obscurity to a sharp weapon,
a detonator, poison, or a gun. Now's the time to make dream
blood run. I see what he's really like when I'm asleep. Entitled
to lead he decrees our loss of substance, gives my gems to rich men.
Gives scarabs I've carved as embodiment of my life's shadows,

commonly taxable, to the ministerial: do you understand this dream?
Destroy him and, too, them. We are spurned as what we really are,
creators of self diamonds, of our essence, I have a diploma
in long breath. I have breathed for decades, enshrining untinctured light.
He can't have it to give away to his colleagues in refurbished
appearances, the old signifiers spruced up as false councils
of reason, care, and change. I want to see the blood from their organs
of entitlement, fuscous and cadenced with clichés, run in her streets.

Two of us, dual case, speaking at once, voiced in the one of her.

We are hostile together but are differently voiced, hostile
to each other, often, but unite in unfriendliness towards top man.
We shore each other up, hating ourselves, each and each other.
Women hate themselves, they say—do men say it? It's what I say,
I eat the road with my head, mouth of ingestion of policies.
Police lights appear as we fly through the death tunnel. Push me along.
Let's turn back before we die. He's been our cop, hasn't he? Yes, they
tell us what's been decided; what dreams mean, what our rights get us
at this time: not his job. I want his job. I want it too, money.
We are still forbidden to lead our lives, to be the leader of them.
He leads us, he says. Let's abolish him now, How, in bright permanence?

I don't want to die with you; want to lead myself. Don't want to die
before I've killed them off. Anyone who'd say what our lives should be.

      I am asleep, aren't I?
We are asleep, multiple voices, plied in layered currents;
      I am not sung, but I sing.
We don't just listen, we perform verbal music for ourselves.
      Music is action, in this night.

We can hear it, as we make it, calling on him to desist—
        I will be myself again.
When were we ourselves? eons and lives ago, a string of pearls.
        I will stand outside and sing.
There is nothing but our voices, dreamed, asymmetrically joined:
        I see your voice, or hear it
joins mine in brown plies near the ocean—river?—Can be either.
        Bend or a twist of hawk's wing.
Plies change, we have mutated now; I or we are different—
        I deepened down in layers,
brown against green banks of the river's flowing blue eye pigment
        I am seeing or singing.
We are instrumental in depth, texture, and becoming real—
        Not to be realer than I know,
but to be the unimagined now, not governed, not a mirror.

I've turned to something else, turned into it. Found the buried lightness.
I think you must mean likeness. No it feels shrugged off, I've lost weight.

Gave it to me, the third. Here in the flaw we are carving into,
go to heaven of skill, all in the new time of day's form's light—

We are the several, we shouldn't get bigger, as a group.

Run and hide together. *They* want our meal. We are so light we hide.
I swallow the darkness at the margin unfashionable of the sea.
Destabilize us a little, we'll like that. Like to regain our balance.

Is there something else we can help each other with? Inhabit me
for a moment, a vein of volition or of self-consciousness,
forget to be despairing of success. I didn't want that, Sky.

In texture someone loves me. In history we're more than guests,
we tie and untie it, with other small rooms full of craftspeople,
I meant, sheer survivors. I'm trying, sworn in for a moment's use,

on the brink of the chiming of the hour. I am not hour or eon.
We are instead details of each of us, obtaining redemption.

I am distressed, in exile
                    by my own choice—
                                        is it a wish or fate?
What did I ever choose?
                    Not to be owned,
                                        by a country or man . . .
Oh citizens are fair,
                    loving themselves,
                                        virtuous destructors,
pulpits of memory
                    call to honor
                                        any moral rumor—
shouldn't we all say
                    the name of love,
                                        the cabbage, the laundry, scalps
hung up there; nostalgic,
                    we can be dumb,
                                        when it suits us to snow
all over the buttoned
                    walls' consciousness:
                                        we'll have no more thought.
Suddenly different,
                    whoever took
                                        my place is who I am.
I am a self exile,
                    or I'm myself,
                                        having loosely arrived.
One day I didn't live
                    anywhere I
                                        recognized as country:

but had I ever known

        white lineaments

                carved, of a city's face

that resembled my own?

        I could leave you,

                aggregate of others,

or I could love you now,

        speaking agree;

            I can never agree,

not knowing what spirit

        in me changes

            me, I can only be its.

Whatever impels me,

      forms me subtly,

            from within is my love.

Our footprints glow in the field—expiration's date's incipiency glows
too—half in love with whizkid death, vermilion jaws of it . . .
Boy had to hide, or was shot, corpses land face down I don't care if you die,
I mean I care but really I don't. Wanting to get to the south.
I'd walk all over you, floor of the skin of the fallen, I mean hole where
you were when you praised god's doped warriors. Let's praise a loaf of dry bread,
crap sausage—I can't eat that—Yes, you can, you're a coherent animal.
Do real people talk like we're talking now? Someone humming Private Lives.
I can't give in to your dream—It's a frazzled fate, honey, a sleight-of-hand
tablecloth, torn but working—DaDah. And your battered conscience disappears.
I got a new eyedropper for a spike. Remember all of this now.
You were our front, took the brunt of those suckers up north. We're everyone's dogs.
It's noise I can't take anymore, can't bear your muddled laughter.
The palisade must be climbed next tonight. Thousands of greased suns will rise.

How can we not have a leader if we are to have this infrastructure?
　　　Let's think about it differently now.
We are in small groups quarreling sometimes because that dynamic pleases:
　　　it's not the same as war with its destruction.
I am always, in part, my friends though there's friction—I don't want to be you.
　　　In my desert free I commingle with sand,
each of us, as is said, universe, all of it. We have digressed too far—
　　　Nothing's too far. The question's how to keep
the electricity flowing without a boss there up on the steel stairs.
　　　We each know how to do things, we just do it.
That simple? Who's ever tried? After all, no one wants the power to stop.
　　　I'm a street person, I don't care if it stops.
Destructure everything you can; don't buy things you don't need. Talk to me.
　　　This conversation reminds me of pilgrims.
I don't want the power to go out, especially in the winter.
　　　Most of us don't want that, we won't let it go out.
We have to trust each other, even if I think I'm smarter than you are.
　　　I am the smartest, but it doesn't matter.
Last night I saw that when I flowed out and became all else I was nothing,
　　　I was everything. We are the electricity.

We are trying to be inside
　　　　　　　Now, our own times, stop naming
us, as if you own all the names.
　　　　　　　　　I couldn't enter, my key
wouldn't fit in the museum lock.
　　　　　　　　　Office of art's closed to me.
Do it on your own like a life.
　　　　　　　　　I want to make some daylight.
There's a pink stain light left above
　　　　　　　　　green uncircumstantial hills.
Hills but no hills remain to us.
　　　　　　　　　We aren't allowed to make hills.
Green like nightshade green, stab-your-heart
　　　　　　　　　　darkness to make you afraid.

What can I fear now I'm a saint?
                              I'd have to fear all being.
They will cut you to pieces, child.
                              I am saintlike not childlike.
Green as the inside of your thoughts
                              where you can't go, they're too deep.
I can't find our times—Don't exist—
                              can't discern the differences
between items called valuable.
                              They're all the same if costly.
Art's all the same on one wall.
                              I'm only saintly because
I'm in another time, the real time.
                              Come with me now to that green.

In my sleep I have contempt for everything that's organized
according to the ancient laws, visual, cognitive, cut.
What has edges? not my thinking. Without another, formless
I am at peace, take care of nothing, extinct; you observe me,
but I'm not even a plain mood. What history was I in?
I've not thought of seeing right since I began to break windows.
I can't direct my gaze, I just see, I just know. Don't save me
from this chaos where any tale, equally, can be entered,
not for forever, or even until its details are clear.

There was a rumor I was now Helen, the crow of this land,
flying over emotional landscapes of cultural trees.
I'd been a skilled kisser but now I carried bugs in my beak.
We were called to you by your beauty but you are sarcastic.
Oh I'm that? How did it come so easily to me, after
I was broken-tongued from the war? Now I can caw, understood.

It is my character dismantled flying, twisted like an iris, blue;
stands in for eyes, for my eyes, the law of the iris has been broken.
I painted but I now see within myself, which is the cosmos.
Cosmos daisy, cosmos iris, I saw him down in the netherworld,
down in myself, I need no iris for the interior world of visions.
He turned to look, flashed his blue eyes, law of the iris broken.
I see how you were swollen with ego or with guilt—whatever we call flaws.
I, am I flawed? How can I make decisions for others, as all men do?
Dead, walked away with dead others, my like, no one like me but we're dead.
Are we now like? Is my character, flawed, dismantled, iris petals torn?
We see, the dead can see, the eyeless irises of blue always see—
you see all night in your dreams. And the blue of my voice can't help but see you.
Walked into death, we mean sleep, we mean internal vision of the eyed self.
I saw the dead, I saw the ones I knew, they looked the same as I knew.

I am invulnerable, voice that doesn't calculate or rage.
I rise up swirling from beneath your thoughts gnawing.
From beneath cells and electrical impulses, from beneath story.
We have to have a story, food or love or war.
Those are our stories. No, there's only a voice from your well.
I wait for it though, story's shape. You're mistaken;
only the voice is you. Wait for the story at a table,
I'm waiting for them—one will wear a charm bracelet.
Marry me says someone to the one wearing it, in Philadelphia.
Your generation bears a story now, it's charmed:
legends for each of you painted on the wall of the second floor.
Do you know what that conveys to a stranger arrived?
For I've become just a voice, absorbing your group voice's meanings.
I have my own self's presence joining you within
the restroom, place of rest. Too much water's being used for flushing.
I like this story but I like my voice better,
deep as it comes from within. I'll follow it to hell, as the wrens say.

Join me, can you walk with me? In this dreaming we move without traction,
    to move is verbal. Have we arrived in some house?
This portrait bothers me, silky dark hair and beard—it's too flat.
    A square to press there, there below in the wood frame.
I know I'll have to recall his meaning when I awaken, but
    now awake I can't. May have been a terrorist.
Do we determine his part? Was he supposed to be another life
    affecting ours more than we affected his own?
We are the determinants of his effect on us. Can we go back
    and press the square, the face of his ticket?
To our own history I mean. Well if he blows you up he's right in it,
    I press the square and he says, I am your knower.
He means we're his knower, to know him the way he wants us to.
    Is this why we exist as more than one of us,
to exalt his life, not ours? It's time to smash the portrait of him.
    I hate to agree, even that far. He simply
has no effect on my mind. Can I have an effect on your mind then?
    Not particularly, and why do you want it?

Vote on your death, citizen, vote for your mind's extinction.
Let's negate life's force in order that we might sleep in tamed hands.
I'm a cold but flowery spring; pretense of being cared for—
you are only *safe*, as in ideas of who you are. Piece
of his democracy. Of his rule. Adamant to cover you
with his own glory and power. He represents all poems.

Can't you forget him? Not for a day, he's over me, but no one
knows who I am. Love is never appeased if she's repressed,
comes from beyond the ocean, causing adults to transform
from the mild sheep of the city, into crazy changelings.
For my love I would not follow rules of his bored marketplace.

This is an ancient history. People fell in love once more.
They forgot to eat, to make money, and they never voted.
They only cried out to me, Love. They had forgotten so long

now they couldn't move without me. Garlanded with hyacinths.

I think to change it by drowning him in the harbor of black piss.
      I want to dislodge bricks of the pyramid,
it's just dust inside anyway, grimacing mummies. They're now fatal
      if you look at them, make their decisions hidden
in windowless tanks. They're just people. No they're ghouls with power,
      and we who are the people don't have any.
We keep all this in place with our good-natured votes. I hate their ideas,
      I don't want somebody else to be thinking for me.
Can't we just leave our jobs? What about the upkeep of these shit apartments?
      We don't know how to do anything alone.
We're always trained to do one lousy thing, that no one needs anyway.
      Tempted to leave and live on the streets alone.
I don't want to do anything I'm supposed to anymore. Quitting.
      I won't band together with you either now.
Fight, you can fight where he sends you, some remote place. Supposed to be hellish,
      mountains and deserts full of danger to us,
thousands of miles away from here. He and his people are dangerous,
      the building's made of dust and can't be repaired.
It's going to fall on all of us anyhow. Go on and prod it.
      Oh I don't care what happens I'm by myself.
Are you? I'm alone now in the derelict wind rushing out to see no person.
      We'll be inside you. Inescapable voice.

Oh spring, it's green, isn't it? Oh the spires of two cathedrals are tall,
I walk between the two—why two? Why anything in a life?
You could be Christ, or Mary; there is no Notre Dame, not for this one—
there is no tall woman, though I wanted to be very tall.
How much have you suffered? It isn't just, is it? No it's not,
two cathedrals full, Christ is you: Wear a dress, says your friend.

Christ is a real man, the tall Dame isn't a woman, just structure.
Once I was tall, now I'm uncertain again, like in college.
I'm glad you're wearing a dress: he says it. Patronizing like a jerk.
There's always someone who makes you be feminine, not yourself.
Heaped shoes and small items, clothes, massive barricades, objects for wear,
as of years of usage. Do I have to remember or something?
Do you remember what you've been through all the time? Not even you.
The churches are too big; I only remember them. I'm cold.
I put on a sweater, a long one, but I'm still chilly, fragile.
I feel a great hatred for these shapes I'm in. Become larger
than them . . . I am larger than you are, am the cathedrals, am I?
Bigger than them, bring it all down, I sure can handle that.

Every voice is real. What can I say? Clinging to your heartroot,
then winding up through throat, I can cry out. Wise I don't occur now,
though suffering rises up and shames me. Ashamed I'm not happy,
poisonous abjection. She could die now; no one would see it, her.

It is an accident that you are well-off, powerful, and content.
Would I feel stronger if I saw you weak? Doesn't comparison
strengthen one? Isn't that how we find out we've been well rewarded?
Dragonflies swarm above pond scum in the sun. Joyous imps ride them.

You don't need to attend to the trappings of the ruling idiots.
Don't you understand them? Engraved features, no despair, chosen skulls—
the elect—stay away. I'm your ancestors in you, impoverished,
energetic simple patterns of motion. Turn your back on those ones.
Avoid monetary values, authorities, people who ride.
You're too old to go back on who you are. Us, the ones with nothing.

Bodiless we don't suffer: in a dream we aren't hungry, don't mourn you.
There is no other in my dreams, no beloved, there's no love . . .
I've been in love in a dream. Have you been in love while speaking, singing?
distorting life you might say, but what is it if not spoken?
The watchers listen more than see. I have no body to see,
I don't care what I say. We've come here to be mixed into one sound,
the dream, or is it voice, of us. I meet you there in the vowel—
we don't have vowels, don't have categories we know in the act of it.
Don't take my voice apart with names. Love is a liquid force.
None of this is true enough. I don't admit you as a rightful judge.
We, the voice, are only unified by being in the same voice.
Who are you as entities then? We are ourselves, that's enough.
Aspects of me or of us? Do you need to know the answer to that?
We're all ourselves, oh voice of us, focus of our expression.

A dreary pedantry would emulate the carelessness of those
who aren't artists, but I speak from before, eons before and they
to whom I refer aren't here in this voice, this vocal projection
where I'm suddenly live, not an ancient. No I'm speaking for you,
you don't know that you're former. But I'm not: my voice is animate,
present, existing. Where are the critics? They aren't here, talentless
their voices are dead. Who are you, in us, disrupting our measure?
Playwright, agitator. Any voice acts in its shaping of sound:
my role of the slave is primary. Anybody can be one,
a slave—is a voice so? Am I slavish? A slave is very active,
works, machinates, and shines, at least in words. Who cannot be free?
Theorist, with verbiage, not a sound. Oh, you're not very dead.
I only want to be alive, untimed. I am dying so young . . .
Always who you were then. Early moment. That was mine forever.

All the evil that concerns us, as women suffer always,
without knowing the difference between their lot and the good,
all that evil happens to me, but so understatedly.
There are times when the air itself seems a concentration camp
for us but not for them, though it's the same air it isn't same
if you're always servile walking, sexed walking or with some name
you never asked for, he beat me. That's a cliché isn't it?
He asked me to give up my show. Told me I knew nothing large
in the same useful way as he, but I could be a symbol.
At some future date, I would be allowed to excel at style.
Reflecting the light faint I wept. He said I was different
from men, without mathematical talent you can't lead us.
You have water in your eyes, what can you see then? Soft caring
you can advocate for your kind, who are too weak to speak well.
My mother was a great woman, and she made me what I am.

The quartz iceberg arrives with kings of the depression stacked on it.
My voice again, nothing changes. Women are not allowed truth,
not allowed speaking roles, not allowed to be precise. They say
in a rhythm of lying, I'm almost equal now, children,
embrace me. When my death comes I'll have nearly been the one.

I see blood sliding like thread, a red strand flowing, there amid the spring snow.
        I think we're toppling him by crying out justly,
but we topple all governments in this space, banishing their altars,
        their archaisms. I am not shuddering,
I'm—we're—darker than that, like to see it, blood, if it's really his.
        Don't think of yourself as a rare sacrifice,
blood has no beauty except in our vocalise, which is not sincere, but
        natively counted. We just count syllables
counting you out; gathered here interrupting work forever in our mouth.
        No one has to do anything, you were wrong.
There is no necessity, I don't like to eat. Welcome to our light clothes.
        Tormented I lurched, walking the street of his need.

His exigencies, his sense of priorities, controlled our times' meanings.
　　　I don't need money, what I need is to speak.
And color in my voice from your presences; others were always there.
　　　Let this blood flow away into the bygones.

One might sense gods everywhere, even within one's own self.
What if I am I but penetrated by divinities?
We have loosed these gods ourselves, they are our finest creation.
They are apart, have their own lives, come like a storm or a bird.
Like a voice mutating to song. I plant my feet on rough earth
waiting for an idea's kiss. Suddenly I'm going home;
I don't have grapes, I have apples. I am capricious, they say.
I am rebellious, or I fear, either in contradiction.
I don't have a casual life, but exist to be possessed
by misery, grace, or laughter. Who can deny there are gods?
There is a god of revolution . . . Can it be within myself
or does it pass from one to one? I'm an individual
prey to deitific visits. But I can't merge with others—
obscene, Bacchic, and abhorrent—too strong a god, like murder—
I will change alone. Do not tax me to combine in anger
with other voices and bodies. Can't I go lonely to bed?

Did anyone ever ask, ask this voice, what is it you want?
No one ever asked me—Or me—what it was I wanted here
on this earth or in this mind that we share as a big community.
The leader asks by shouting words: if we shout back we agree,
that's called demagoguery. I'd like to be asked what I want here.
What is it that you want? I want to know things and to love.
I want this economic and political structure to collapse soon.
That will be so painful for us. As painful as mourning is?
I want to know why my loves had to die. Who cares for money? fools.

We invented money when we could have invented the gift.
I want to wear a hibiscus. I don't want to be a decent
person of the middle classes. Don't want to be prosperous—
Don't want to live in a house with a lot of rooms and solar panels.
I don't want anything at all. I have no wish. Not to work.
I don't want to see his perishable face printed on every surface.
I want sunlight, clear air, and silence. I want brains and a thought.

There is nothing here now, there is only me.
This is black void here now, there is just my voice.
There is black emptiness, there is nothing here.
There isn't anything, I am appearing.
I am nothing but sound, first I am a voice.
If there can be nothing, something first sounds.
Hi hoo ho hoo something, hi hoo ho hoo some.
I am not a person, nor am I a god.
I am making the world by creating sound.
I am not existing, I have a brownish face.
I am not present, I'm only a voice.
There is black emptiness, out of which I chant.
I begin creation, but I'm not a god.

And then you are someone. First I was voice. Crying? No I made sounds—
metrics were the first sounds in the cosmos. Oh, that's ridiculous.
There was a face just materialized, so it could chant poems.
The voice demarcated patterns of sound; poetry is living—
I am composed of mathematical proportions, equations,
I am composed of poetic structure. I am a voice of lines,
without this measurement I'd not find you. Must we find each other?
The first chant is raw words: I don't know them, they're from another tribe.
Yet I said them in a sense: for I was there. It was only a dream.

All I've ever wanted was to hear that. He had a maiden's hair coils:
he was not gendered, nor was he there. Only the sounds were there.
Hi hoo ho hoo sounding, hi hoo ho hoo sound. But that wasn't really it.
I was there at the beginning, inside I'm there potentially
always: poet and ear. All measurement stems from this first moment.

Tell me voice, do you have values? Who knows? Come apart in my mouth.
Values wait for your tweaking, call your name. That's when I try to leave.
You're just in from your birth! We don't need ways. We don't want bright futures,
I'm not that person now. It's not random, but it's not what they said.
I told him I wouldn't vote. You're a woeful pullulation like that,
cry out for power when we're all entwined, an electricity,
reconfiguring charge, jolt of juice. We were not reborn to vote—
I choose darker sounds. Don't you want part? Automatically
you kick in with a hiss. I like it when you want to argue hard,
deceptive asterisks spit out of space while you shriek at us all.
Messages are uncertain, but not joy. So you keep talking there.
The earth of the strangers. When I arrived, this time, we had no roots.
Just as well, it's so red here at the dawn, I'm moving in with chimes.
Do you like clarinets? I like walking. This is different now.

If I don't move nothing happens. Incurring obligation
is my enemy now, eating is, needing anything's bad.
But you still need us, the voices. Yes, we're remaking the world
as it collapses from its wrongheadedness and lonely
disclaimer of spring. It thinks change is a return to former
strangeness, when we loved money for what it could buy not its blue
haze of glamour around our throats. I don't seem to have enough.
Let's have something else, a pulpit, frail, made of forgetfulness.
I don't remember how to speak for myself anymore,

only for us, members of voice, deciding how to go on.
Our pitiful savings are in his bank of ghosts, bar-drunk men—
bar between us and all of them, well-being of their houses.
Perfect wives of interesting sexists say they know something,
how to be wealthy and brave. I'd just as soon shoot them both.
But I won't, I like it in hell—I always have. No one
ever comes around to disturb my reconciliation
with the eternal magicians, power of my transforming.
Some of your voices are them, aren't you? We're changing our whole life.

Trying to match metrics
                    to a room in an apartment I'd sell
I feel the line attached to me,
                I embody it, I'm obsessed
or am I now made over?
              I will sell you these rooms we've made of us,
long and empty, light, matching our sound
                  to an externality,
we can arrive at vision.
            There was speech first then we saw where we lived;
bodies and houses—they're fluid,
            this is a beginning state.
Everything spoke the same tongue,
            or they say, the traditional peoples—
can we understand each other,
           now in this late first language?
I have measured the new world
           from within, envisioned it with my own line.
Will you purchase this apartment?
           I can see it needs windows.
All of the plants, animals,
         minerals outside speak the same way too,
or else we wouldn't be in the
        same world together, you know.

I know the apartment
                    suits my temperament. And what is that?
A forceful impression of things
                    as we make them and speak them.

Beauty's what I want now.
                    I look for it
                              within and without my-
self, when I feel serene
                    that's beautiful,
                              when I see forsythias,
when someone reads poems
                    I exist to
                              be the one who's feeling it.
It isn't for me in-
                    dividually,
                    I am the universe
as senses for beauty,
                    or as beauty;
                              no need for forgiveness,
drama, or oppression—
                    watch lights appear
                              through the trees at evening
while your daddy cleans fish.
                    It's all that's left,
                              only in memory
as I'm you, the voice who
                    remembers me,
                              there used to be a world.
It was my legacy;
                    I'm not a small
                              body. I'm the whole thing,
I'm alive and dead now,
                    at the same time,
                              speaking in your poems.

Who are we together? I'm pursued by Eumenides, Furies—
are they part of all us? Are they projections from my own mind or
yours in hatred of me? Huge bloody moths, clawed, they whine stupidly
so I can be stupid. These are modern versions, close enough, keep
me from your group, they're my commune; not real, they render me unreal:
do you remember everything you've done, or only what you wish?
I remember nothing, I'm just fearful, of my memories, but
they keep me busy, these black curses, making me bleed, not think.
I can't join you except when they're asleep. Classical plight, humans
always pretending you don't know what it is to kill another—
horrible, sending me off to do it—casting me out from you
first to defend your investments, then take responsibility
for your mute decisions. Be your actor. You're too lazy, passive
to suffer: I do that for you too. Here's our society,
there are you, and there's me. And there are they, almost voiceless wonders.
Can they join the chorus? They're so loyal; attach themselves like dears.

We've collected all of us figments or fragmenta, even the Erinyes, even enemies,
even those we can't face. We don't have faces except for an internal glimpse as we
remember how I'd once seen you, mixed with how you're changing,

for you're transforming yourself as we intermix, voices without color? I remember
blue, now I see it cobalt. I see your eyes as you say how you hate my voice, you say
you always hated how I treat you.

Is that a part of our new way of existing? You don't have to tell us how you used to
feel—I still feel I hate her. Change for you're bigger composed of so many strands, all
of us but alone you're someone entranced by your true borders.

I was once ruled by hard custom, now I'm defined by converging beings within my
voice, my territorial range. I am the one behind me, can you understand each of us is
like that? New since I now see, I'm remade as clarity.

No one has spoken for me, for long decades though I'm thought depicted
        in the cultures of, oh, I see some smoke we'll eat
sold in the wind of cinema, the downloaded jingles of buzzards.
        These birds can't sing, they croak their lustful insolence.
I haven't known what I've felt since those cons started selling me feelings.
        I like to use my voice here; though it's yours, it's mine.
For I have wrath and courage equal to an actor's or popstar's.
        I'm smart as a professor in that I'm alive,
remaining so without tenure or fellowship: I'm a fellow
        and credible within myself, the one who cares—
the one who sings and who acts, in our version of culture and the ride.
        It's mine, I'm mine, I won't pay them to be my glass.
We are our mirrors here, speaking songs by lamplight of intellect
        not separated out, given to the special ones.
I'm creative and smart as the distance of collapsing governance,
        I just want to say it: I knew what was coming.

        I'd rain on you if I were rain,
hard, watching you look defeated because I'd like that,
        wouldn't I? Or do I care now?
But I like the old themes, temptation, vengeance, hate.
        Maybe I don't feel anything.
Shit drifts through me wanting to be a thought of mine,
        I don't need the aggravation.
Get some convictions, man; don't be a scrawny brain,
        all you do is sweep linoleum.
I like floors, and I don't want to defend something.
        I get dust into a good pile,
then it's gone, remember cleaning compounds? looked like
        tobacco, remember smoking?
I'm not going to defend this shitass democracy,
        it damages me with its trash—
its ideas are trash, blatantly showing off:
        I can sling it, he says with pride,

And that's what we're about, conventional big words
        red and olive not green. Well it's
still Christmas and someone gave me a theory
        of economic recovery.
I didn't want one, I wanted a bird call whistle.
        I'd like some intrigue now, a spot
of birdsong on the wall, wings in shadow flutter,
        explain that, you dummy, a thought
in my mind sings the one thing I want sounding here.

Who are the people? I am not a crowd of fire.
I'm not a victim of weather; I'm perhaps a city's face.
The youth grows older; dried up limbs are holy,
since it's the people who know that rags will age and die by rote—
our bosses, thinking, don't. They emphasize their brains,
naming each other cunning, as if they thought the gods were theirs,
employed as loyal aides, but gods do as they will
emptying banks; if they think your thought is arrogant, reading
your mind they become it, tricking you to fateful action,
avarice is a god's trap—he laughs at you because you're had.
The people's voyage takes them past the isles of greed,
stupor of hooking deceit, but stalls in the the seas of vengeance:
I need to kill you who upset the flow of grace,
flow of the small ways we love within a life that's difficult—
your wars, your wages, your disastrous economy
always end up as our weight: then we must pull you down again,
we'll gore the lot of you, we'll spare no one up high,
burning the white house of liars: the gods now possess all of us.

Now I, voice's owner, must speak for me, if that's possible—
I keep identity as a body letting you in my heart—

and I see we're the same on the level of intelligence here,
educational fingerprints vanish, because we're essential:
I shape your speech but you always say how you exist and reflect . . .
We reflect each other, thinking, and you. You are the only one,
though, who speaks for us all, we the people: you're our emissary,
from us to us and you. I seem to love you, though I never see you.
Love's practical for us; a tone of voice. We are free here, but we
should be free in our lives. We don't want others to guide us, ever,
except in our groups of the several, one might accept a hand;
we want to reject all politics, in our conscious living,
if we can transfer this voice from our sleep outward to our waking
motions, our walking around as humans. As if our voice flowed down
into our limbs, out through eyes and marked fingers picking fresh flowers.

Oh my lord or lady, within my heart—sayeth the old voices—
we remember our words for the lover, in us of ruffled forms
to summon eros forth, within the same elemental longing
grace is consigned to. I walk in thick substance or force visual,
tactile as a sticky, universal basis of how we'll act,
vocal light-limbed beings—having departed from enslavement's trance
when we thought that love was subservience. We are each lady, lord.
There is no other love, this very one, speaking in our letters
I see and shall be heaven to a one, growing as crystal trees.

We leave mere credulity of merchants, enter into touching
power of articulation's diamonds liquefied. It's your mouth
kissed, kissing what was previously thought to be disorder of serfs.
We are all that there is, unclassed and whole, motion of clear sweetness.
Each one we are equal; without a star fating us we're in spring.

We are the ones who make things, bring this world into focus, then let it trail into
wisps of chaotic edges. Do you speak of what's within you, or of the agreed world?
I, am I I, speak now of how we together define it, but it's within as well—
we the people are a defining principle, aren't we? We are the consciousness.
I am my own consciousness. I don't want to be part of you. But you are, aren't you?
Another way to say it: we are each the whole thing, and I merge with you when I wish.
You don't create, by yourself, world of speaking, world of our jointure, by definition—
Oh but I need my lone self!—How we love that in your oeuvre!—Don't want to be
      loved . . .
Yes, yes I do; but each one needs to be still sometimes, not speak. Is that to be alone?
I'm courting chaos in me. But you want to shape it, don't you? Let it flow through my
      mind.
Maybe it's us; as alone, we are unformed, have no leadership within our minds.
This is a very strong place, seize on it becoming new, or would it be ancient?
Chaotic to cast out kings: chaotic within cast him out. Strength to be grandiose
without an order in place; mountains have no edges, the clouds, I mean the clouds are
      them.

And in time armies fall apart. Disbanding from inertia—
      that hasn't ever happened—
it happens now in this expanse. How? Everyone comes to us.
      Here, in the night, unconscious
come the soldiers with blurred voices: If we don't live here we'll die,
      souls will die, of despair—
I was not born to be worse than other animals for him.
      Why should we kill each other
so that he can have a book deal? That is the logic I'd serve.
      Why should we be laid off now
so that he can solve our problem, take the credit historically?
      I have come here to be us,
to be myself and to choose you, choose a stream of harmless words
      riding it, lotuses
on the pale river under moon mild with our lovable change.
      All the soldiers are coming,

seeking our voices to be free; I see you with my finesse
        of cajoling sentiment,
a vocal talent, not a con; it's for your dark appeasement.
        This is where you must live now.
We have left the battlefields. Our doubles continue, but
        they're too empty to fight on much
longer. I couldn't bear to stay, there in my body of arms.
        I had always been valiant,
hadn't I? I wondered if I had to have a character,
        characteristics: brave, skilled,
so that others would die of it. They weren't supposed to be my
        conscience, twisting in the sand.
I don't know what's the point of it, being; I just got sick of his face.

They ran it without the top levels; they walked away gradually
from the top people, taking the rest with them; I mean we did that—
we left them, for we ran it all didn't we? were the technicians
vocal in truth, voices of the larger part, it. Aren't we it?
We can run it; left them. Left all their wars. We just disbanded the
high levels not only of government but of big companies
we worked for, we kept making goods when boss ceased to pay; we need goods
not money; the army, sick of war, had joined us. It just happened
without thinking of it. The climate gone, and leaders had nothing
to acquire but dust; we need to live. Power over the dust?
Was the new world a good? We should have broken up with them eons
ago; it's deserts, it's flooded-out cities no one leads—they're muted
the former top men—always so much to do—in this future you
see now with your voices; try to help us; you the past led us here . . .

FOUND WORK
(lost lace)

▫

If caught in ending you may understand
that time is magic locked I put in here
        it always comes from nowhere, though
    the words are already formed

I wasn't any person any more. the words
        would say. they
    do as they please

don't eradicate me, as if I were a culture

    the word
    the clawed and golden
        hand
    that holds you up from her grave site

    but
    my witch never sleeps.
        I never sleep

This injury, beautiful being
this apocalyptic need for magic
        obviously predicts my face
    has resulted in a blank dress and
throat disc

        river predicts my
    face where the sun shares its blood

            shot in
            the head
        when the flood
    comes or dries up

across a planet once owned by advances

That man's butterfly over his dead
    extensions
        called me back from hell. I don't
care where I
         am, this one-thing
  world
      is the dirtiest thing
love's the dirtiest thing in the world

      they're
dumping my works on the street to
    have my
  rooms and that's a future

    then along tops of cliffs impersonating
mass movement of creatures a line
    that's you. Are you prepared to
lose everything
        and be one with
  your fellows
      a migratory wound
now that there's only one
           genocide

When I step into this
position of power
                    I must stop
            caring, to help.
It is the reverse of the
            late-form presidency: I
            the dark
    am really in charge
            of the device
In order to effect a change I
    can't care
                    camerado
        who you are. or pretend to

I won't bring us together

    I am giving you yourself. take it

It's not that the planets are put out one by
one—the stars, the lights
     as they are said once to have been
turned on

     But this is a story of the end. don't
you want to hear it
                           no you want
  your wife
    who is always young, so much
    younger than you

Identify with me as your
        soul. come among the old
    battles
                fire where heads melt who's
        had a thought since
                        Shoot the motion
    you fear
                    out of the treasured ways taught
    across the grim
    sea. The
    young man says he is always
                            blood-spattered
    absent-hearted in the skeletal eras of our
        cultural conceit.
No one may be left to dig up our femurs
    our significant rings our weapons our
                            manuscripts for
        in more ways than war we
    are killing ourselves; who have
        nothing to live for except the approval of
        our flesh-eating god

I'm not who I thought
I'm not there or here
it's anywhere
in the broken clock
there's no
solar system
because those words   solar   and   system
are broken with the breaking of the
climate who will know
the words we made for what we saw
when there's no sight

A gold flower, a brown and gold flower
an old fabricated
     form

  drying gold
       mental
       chrysanthemum

    lovely—for I had made it with my
eyes—and some words inside
        my gutted self see figure p. 2

    There was no reason in what happened

      there are no flowers

I disavow any reason but ink on
   paper to be viewed in the future
   by no one

Talking to you, who can't be.

Someone rock and gold–
              red light
      I am the one
You
      wanted me
            to be dead. as dead as you
      I had always   gone along

Sun and shadows,

      Not bothering to remember
our importance our wars our words
      for our terrifying crimes
      oh weren't we everything

Gone I'm still supposed to be
      you and your symbols
I'm supposed to be as you imagined
      our earth
      Well you broke it your concept
and now I'm the
      one alive
I'm always alive

By default, since there's no one
    else here
I am your soul. what you know
  in this place. But we're dead
or you're dead; I can't be—
    I am your
manuscript speaking. the only woman
    in town.

Obviously predicting my face where
the sun shares its blood
        they would arrive
                            at night
to sleep outside.
                They say
    they are left over
The women and children are leftover things
        he leads you to hard places to lie down

    If you remember better times
you know they were lies, because they led
        to this

She lies flat on a bier or bed
crystals spring up from her midriff
    I have nothing left to tell but these
rocklike things
             pressure
  part of our nature baby

        you might still call
what happens fortuna, or
  "then reasoning fell apart"
I'm going to save you because I am
a word.

    The heart from which crystals spring up
      what are they for
    Flawed to ask

They thought they were greater than
shadows
    some because they could think
  or something like that (who cares now)

He created an intricate argument to
  prove that there's no foundation
                I'm sleeping on
    Inside of
couples
   crying out, We deserve sexually
  that the wheel stay stopped

  forgot that Fortuna—there is no
  fortuna—thinks in as ghostly a
  (doesn't think) way

The story that I fall in love again
in the middle of apocalypse
    or after massacre—details?—no
Someone still wanted me to bind or cling
there was a dress, black and pale yellow so
    I could be her
    but I said I wasn't
        I was this page

Some ideas might have been useful:
Certain forces are damaging
        (lightning strikes you) others
are good. the sun
    was formerly good
there was a balance. the human must
    approach this balance
scrutinize it—and herself who mirrored
        it—for extremes, acute disharmony.

Natural harmony collapsed
because the prayers (scrutiny)
    no longer invoked balance; the

environment appropriated as
    personal power, as tool (and so
not respected) became unbalanced:

nothing but heat, or
    nothing but water; men were
witches without knowing what that was.

    But I, the page, know what a witch is
and am one
    being both a possessor of
"natural" power and a medium of transformation

The mood of the last plays

    trying to become inorganic
One time.
               trying not to be bound
into a night
                 Can evolve into what I
haven't thought

(the only thing we can do)

    be careful or you lose your
                      Reflex
pointless to have a
           mood so what do we have
I'm not trying. there's nothing can
                   take me
people can't force me any more

I'm
  still with beauty (on the side of)
               like luster
               can you *have* it

    what was lost to the collective
hurt
       ownership of contractual scars
what a human was supposed to get
    all the ways to wear time
        scars on my mind
                 gone

Scarlet it can't be a flower
  and so it isn't

It was in another life, it was in another
culture
                    draw near to the town crier
    he deals a complicated blow of words

I don't remember how I used to feel
    inferior
                to some
            haphazard fortune
                to some
    that haphazard fortune had given arms
        of aggressive argument
    it was the words of nothing to see
        the crier and his blind wife
        for I foresaw being this page left
            buried

            Blond dark glasses over-
            weight hair pulled back,
            dancing in front of a dusty tree
            near the sno-cone palace

    If she was our venus
                        our tumescence
        last of the latinate deserts
        wearing circular dark glasses
                it kills her
                kills her

    our spirits flying out everywhere

In the times of loving we possessed
    each other and land, we possessed
rich words, I mean
we owned companies and real estate
    homes wardrobes everything
another might want
                          machines to
    communicate our desires or
to transport us so we might appear
    before others in fine clothes
and with a chosen mien.

If everything's done for seeming
    then there isn't anything
the blood thick
        all footholds shaken
    killed for resources and religion the ex-
cuse so that women might never be fully
human
        as one condition all enemies assented to
    Thus I am not a human
        And as the world device has broken
not from war but from the action of our
    machines so necessary to seeming
better and stronger than others,
    I speak only to show you my lack
of common humanity
            but am still interested in
    power
        as being what there is.

Given that I am force or power
in a shape we have previously called mortal
my identity as person is a misattribution
the cosmos being composed of
        locations of what there is:
    identical, unique.
A variety of multiple zoning
        It is horrible how people
decided what they were.

    There were three sisters each composed
of people pushed into
        a form of dress pattern
    with finely scrolled collar
and sleeve forms
                    so they could exist there
                            in the patterns
there were complaints

    Now that the world is over the sisters
are brownish yellow colors
        Identity of view from within
    she is a color gradient
we are still modeling ourselves on supposedly
                            perceived
        outer particulars
    but the language of that is falling apart.

I am willing myself—you have to
walk down the stairs—apparently to
   descend and embrace that man—but I
don't have time—who is ascending.
   He always
      had to go up.
                        What is the
point of this kind of contact
      at the great commemoration,
               but I knew there would
soon be so few that the "great" part
   was transitory
moment.
                     There had once been a poet
and we were supposed to envelop our-
selves in the splendor of that man
      But it was already too hot
            I am coming down
internally, you have found the
   people of which you are one
   wanting
               so why do you participate
in the manuscript
                        For its beauty
   I was gold in it not like a person
                  But
      every night people, people
in a crowd are what I dream about
      claiming
my old alive space a burglarized
   store. I could replace the locks
      went out
      barefoot instead and
            gave it to them
                        Magically I
keep going to other space (what
   else is each page)
                  they follow me

With
an ancient harmonica
      I got to be man wrong
            be man wrong.

The old man built a slump upon
      his back; he became
Wrong Mountain. Why not?
            if everything's already
there it didn't happen
And hence show features
      I don't have to
      I am not in your eyes
Magic isn't easily identified

The golden veins
      of view
      of view and amount
      it's all smudges not even memory of
when you were a couple and
      huge faces stared in at you if
   you didn't pull the miniature
      curtains closed.

               You are
it, power
   choosing to appear in this moment
not looking like anything but
   you because we are rapidly for-
getting our teachings.

I didn't know if I was the damaged
person or he, the damaged person, was
    I mean the cat. of course no person
    I mean the cat I carried to safety
who had been damaged by exposure
                I mean I
was damaged—I can't tell but I
must be the damaged now creature I carried
    for I was exposed to these
treacherous
    elements
            I screamed because the dead
could hear me—they
    were just asleep
first I screamed and then I
        carried the cat to shelter but it
suffered from shock, which was orange
                            electricity

    inside it
    too exposed
but when I'd screamed, the air was blue

                    I'm not
expressing lost narrative
                          I'm the one who
  came back from hell, liking the sound
of whatever I said. This isn't
     hell? No it's paper that you're
   inside, inside me
   a damaged manuscript

     A lot more cultures become rocks
Keep finding me whatever you are
     constant state of disintegration and
          hardening
You will soon become familiar with
     most of the interesting minerals
     calls to me longingly the climate
of replacement
        calls,
               "you broke the solar system"

IF THE REAL IS SO REAL WHY ISN'T IT

I tried to learn how to be a person
in order to be a poet. but I failed,
or I was failed. Too many of
my people died, and I was left
empty of them and then of personal
reaction, as we have been taught
through the ages, and even of personal
event. I feel this was done to me
by unseen powers, so I could be
exactly this way, for you my reader.
I am void of what you would expect.
But it's you whom I love, not other
poets, or most people I can see. Why?
I was designed to be this one, for thee.

Can I talk to you as if I didn't know how?
I have this . . . this grail. It's white with
light, as white as an animal. You can
drink light from it, if you want to. Why
would I? Then you won't fall to pieces
from serving others, as you have been trapped
into doing. As I serve you. I write too fast,
because it's hard to say. And I might not
get all the light in, if I don't hurry. I'm
trying to invent a new language; I was told to
by someone who doesn't exist. Forgive me
for being like this, but I think I should be.
Is this the new language? If you understand
it and like it; though it's old; but I know I'm shocking
someone; and someone will say, What is this?
and someone will say, I get it, but I don't want it.

Do you know what it's like to be transparent?
I'm not particularly interested in anything
but say the first thing that comes to mind.
You of course aren't here, you're where you are.

I sound like something I've heard before.
But where would the words come from? We
believe so touchingly in language acquisition,
enculturation, inculcation, and imitation;
I remember trying to be myself. Now I feel
I was inserted into life exactly not to do that.
For I have been robbed of everything that made
me social: lovers, certain close family—and I
have been ill, too; I think it's desired that I have
not much but words. What good would that do?

The new language is that of explaining these facts.
So far. The human condition is not what any-
one has said. There are forces in charge of us
that have never been named. And will I
name them? I will name something; and it
will then be real. Effable and known to you.

I'm going to sit here a moment longer with
my grail, then leave to mail a letter, to
help procure money for this light, though
money is fake and light is the pervasive
but clichéd as a . . . as a self. I'm
trying to remember something to tell you;
he strung up a small machine, to "help
me plan all my flights," last night in a
dream. It has planned this one, I hope . . .
He suspended it over one of my former beds.
Perhaps because someone died in it; though
I am being born,
                    as I backtrack in my body,

to a more infantine self, when I could just speak.
I hope for love, for how could I not, if I am
in a human body? But I'm unique and a wind

is only what tells me to say. Anything I say
will be used against me, and so I must perfect it.
Are you a woman or a child? I'm smarter than
anyone I know, in a sense. What sense? I'm
detached from you, and I see you succumb to
easy answers and reactions, belittling others.
It is raining words, it never rains, in

the desert where I am being trained. And if
you see her tell her it's broken; I will.

Tell me the words for your problem, and you say:
I don't know how to deal with loss; I fear
death; and others don't treat me well. For
they are deficient in sympathy—the wind
once ripped it out of them—a hot desert wind—
and left them desirous to torment me, as if I
were hurting them, simply by projecting
my own heat out into the open. Aren't
you ever specific? Only words specify:
the tenderness of being alone in a body:
a human couldn't be more vulnerable.
A coyote near an acacia is freer than I;
she can run caring for herself, eating
hardly anything, healing her own wounds.

What she says is aoooo oooo oooo ooooooo!
all my childhood hearing them. Never a child.
These words:

I will tell you who you are, souls hidden
by the manners of tigers and sycophants,

of desires someone named once and told you to have.
I don't want to have a manner. I still love
you, for I see your soul, white as a grail
shaped like a penguin: from a cold place.
For I can be cold, can you? *like* cold. I
observe you with ice eyes sometimes, so I
can see. You need to think of who you really are.
Alone. So you can fulfill yourself by not
doing. Don't do things: they are futile
in the wind, or in the coldest ice, in which . . .
in which you can only carve a grail; you
made it yourself, you know? You did, you.

The ones who are shaping my lifeline secretly
or yours,
    so that I can say "yours"—I thought I was
so selfish. They placed me in my experience, so I would
speak thus to you. We are something like elders,
they say; something like the dead; something
like the wind; and we are you, too. Are you
trying to help? We are who we are. You
are the poet, though; or perhaps, the reader;

the language, the former one, will kill you.
Speak plainly, or be as odd as you need to.
All language comes from us, of whom you are.
It is for you to speak, and think; the dead are
alive, speaking. Among the acacias. The grail
is your ability to live poetically. Everyone.
We invest ourselves in your lives, why?
It is a grail. You heal your suffering, as you
drink of it; it is pure spirit, as we are
singly and together. We chose you to say this,
but we didn't know what you would say.

I was always pushed towards this place.
Or backwards. Sitting in the sand there; wind,
a little. Tell me. The grail is burning now.
(The river's icy.) I'm handing it to you
to be burned. Hold it against your chest.
It's your old-fashioned heart, also it's
your knowledge, that nothing has been named.
Maybe the acacias. The language comes every time.
So you can be alive, forever, you my reader.
In death we speak, in dreams we speak,
and in the immaterial past and future our vocal cords
are fast as birds. I'm calling to you. I have to;
they are making me. Or I am making me.
There is nothing that is dead if there's a grail.
Keep it. Keep it for yourself. I will.

I hear someone say, You should say it in a way
that I like. This is the way I have today. I'm
very young, too young to have another way.
I'm about four; I speak very well. There's a wind
here, but it doesn't help. But I like it, because
it moves. The acacias have their language,
and the sand. I think I understand it. I'm
giving all I am to all of this. It's for you.
We are the ones there are, and will always be.
Do you believe this? you say. I'm too young
to believe, I know. This is uncanny, you
say. The universe is uncanny, I say.
And that's the best word. It's the new.
I'm going to slip into the river and cool off.

THE WIND

It to take; or was it to be unpacked?
Packed it might signify death. The wind
Death the wind calculating your lesson—
hast thou learned a thing? The name of
a thing. I am still defiant, of the pre-
sumption, as articulated. I passed him
in his velveteen jacket worn elbows. The
enculturated elbows of Death need patches.
Do you want my job? he said, for you are brave.
And you are the one different one . . . How do
you know? In your sleep I approach you
and you breathe on me, as if I were an object,
observable malice. I mean, he said, when you
die, that's when you can be me. Spy then thief
always the one left; but then there's more.
I'm too wild, I say; I'm an American. May-
be I'm leaving—for where? bankrupt in
June, lost identity, lost shortcomings.

BLINDING, THE WHITE HORSE IN FRONT OF ME

Blinding, the white horse in front of me. If I ride on it . . .
Have you forgotten yourself enough to come with me?
Hurts so—That's just loss. This hole within—

up we ascend past the constellations of dawn, zircons
still showing: not possible: *this* isn't possible.
I've been here before—So begins my song. I know who
I am. I've been ages striving to exist, but that's nothing.
I am a being calling to morning after the end of all
revelation full of hate and gaudy profit—

I am someone who couldn't find her place, because
I saw that the coordinates had tumbled. My body
coheres but I'm not there, I'm here with this horse
not house, with this speed. Dark trees around,
pale sky, no details—who needs them? There's
no meter in this journey culminated, no sound at first . . .

Then the white steed flames and flares its mane—
I've brought you here to speak, perhaps to chant.
There will be a patient to heal, maybe it's you.

I see a cerise orange hue behind the black paper glen:
I am a seer and a tongue, spelled drum:
Why doesn't it beat *properly*? Time is finished, dear.
I am a being descended from the stars before
the Greeks nailed down their stories. I'm a being
from before the sciences claimed a larger hole
than my mouth—it is my mouth that time crumbles in,
spat out like old words. I am being trembling now . . .

I am the being who rides flame, with one ruby
in her ear. My forehead is wider than a life.
My eyes see past mores; past the nooses of norms.
I am the being whose body is robotic on earth
but floats to heaven, the passion of sleepers, freed.
I am the being who heals, because I'm

the one that doesn't know. I'm the being who
doesn't sleep, the form of this intransigent
setting that doesn't exist and won't go away,
matitudinal ghost-grey sky, spook love.
Do you have a spine? The ladder my horse and I
climbed: of old holocene ivory rungs, up
the aquamarine void. My skull above,
emptied of memory chains that streak away,
worms of nerves. I can heal you, because I'm here.
I am the being who has no notion if it isn't
an image, floating in space, unseen by eyes,
seen by mind as all. I'm the being for whom words
are soft or adamantine, coarse or silky, smeared
or dancing like insects of onyx, of sardonyx,
of bloodstone, and carnelian. I'm the being who
knows no night or day, I'm the one who has no
small feelings; the one who doesn't bleed; doesn't
shit. The being whose horse has a pink tongue;
the being whose horse has past deaths;
the being whose horse forgets all but the word
I am free. The being whose horse doesn't serve me,
but rides here for joy and in my company. I am
the being who heals, because I don't move now. I'm
the being who finds the patient amid all the projections
from ever, where we once sat lamenting. I will
heal you, I will heal you of your evil, your illness, your fate.

This is the patient's soul approaching. The shade lies
down on the ground by the fire never lit but burning
orange with sparks of phosphorescent green. The
patient, genderless, bodiless, will tell me of its anguish:
I feel like an old, opaque secret. I keep asking to be renewed.
I suck on every fad, like mushrooms on a cemetery slab.
Everyone's better than I am; I'm the imprisoned best. No one
loves another except as a mirror to a musty guest, to take
stingy control. We are all failing, masterfully, because we
desire it. Want to see civilizations ruined, want to see our
species' death, our psychic embroidery unraveled. We want
to find out who's left, the impossible perceiver of our demise.

I'm hungry, I'm sick, I'm wounded. No shirt. So tired.
I want to go home. They're killing us; can't remember
childhood. The animal, bloodied, fails to hunt again.
Our genocides are a cliché, repeated, but there's no satiety,
and further horror is willed. Who will save you? Who wants to be
saved . . . I didn't mean to say . . . I didn't mean to be born.

How do I heal you; arching back with gems for eyes,
cut like a fly's into hundreds of facets? I can only
repeat what I am. Lurch forwards, sit and again:

I'm the being who wears different glasses, for I
was the other child. I have made myself different eyes,
to see down the infinite alleyways the universe dissolves
into, at each ecstatic footfall, if you don't care. I'm
the being who sees beyond what you do to me, what I
do to myself, as we multiply a self everywhere. Lice
for all the facets of my eyes. I am resisting music.
I'm the being that resists trance. I'm not in that
trance, I'm above it. I'm the being that resists thought,
for thought is the robot too; I'm the being who can't be sad.
I have never been unhappy, I have never acted, have
never supported a politics; I have never taught a thing.

I'm the being who isn't planetary; we have traveled
beyond our world, to sit in a paper forest lit by jewel-light.
I'm the being out of whose mouth. I am the one
who made the sun; but I don't care about that.
I'm the being you can change into; fire, you are previous
and future. I am resisting grace. I am resisting
goodness; I am not resisting futility, violence, or power lust.
I am absorbing them and spitting them out in these words.
Do these words go anywhere? Go where there is no place.
I enter the image, where there is no changing of hours:
It is outside time that you heal.

Walk with me outside time. You don't have to move your
feet. What walks? Nothing wills walking; over the yellow-image
ground towards more dull black trees. We always wanted

to be here, where creation is effortless. It is my body, but
it doesn't really move, it impersonates motion, so you'll
get it. There are diamonds in here, floating; there are
rubies in this thicket, for your affection. This could be death;
since it isn't anywhere you're supposed to be: outside
your other body, who can you be? You are like me.

And if roses imbued with carbon are what we love,
you say, and if frogs and tigers are dead, and honeybees,
small blue California butterflies, and any number of beautiful
creations, what good is this imagination?

My eyes grow more empty, my mouth gapes:
And all of that destruction belongs to you.
The destruction can't be healed, we are murderers.

I am the being who wears murder like a blazon;
I am the being who lives covered in shiny maggots,
the transcendent dead self-victim, blood-smell
body; I am the being who watches the dance
of naked skeletal prisoners; I am the being who sings
triumphantly to all the dead lovers outlived; the
ghastly wolf who eats any flesh; the commandant
who severs his soldier's limbs; the woman who
razors the clitorises of girls; who else would I be? It's all
in my mouth—loveless. I am the being that
absorbs you—nothing. You are nothing that stays.
I can forget you instantly, or heal you of universal felony.

This is a picture of time stopped: my sense-holes
are empty. Yours will never be unless you become me.

I am the being with no face, inside each animal,
monkey, lizard. Inside the sunflower. If you kill
them as species, you kill me, but here I'll be, dis-
passionate, outside time. Be like me. I am the being
that deflects change, for change is boring and haunted,
the same gestures in shifting colors. You know
all the colors. Stop, just stop. Nothing suffices but

timelessness. You terrify me, you say. I am the being
beyond terror, beyond extinction; details flow off me. Here
it rains a mechanical grey vapor, if that's what
you want. I am the being containing no organs, nerves,
or other definition. I am the being who isn't speaking,
the one who doesn't speak a language, the one
who has no charms or amulets, the one who can't
be bought: you have me so you can't have me.
I'm the being in which the universe is outside harmony,
outside symmetry and consequence. Outside protection.
You have not passed beyond fear; you're shaking.
I have to help everyone; I have to leave, the patient says.
You'll never leave me now. You're mine. Be as I say.

I'm the being who is unfertile; the being with a bloody shield,
I am a skeleton. I have a skull with an artifice of fire in its eyes.
I'm a skeleton enduring past genitals, I am any stick figure
seen beneath the eyelids; I'm your perceptions, shuddering.
I'm the being that won't shudder. I'm the skeleton in
the black robe, with dirty silver stripes, clawed by a cat.
I don't care if I heal you. I place skeleton fingers on your
shoulders; I would never comfort anybody. I'm the being
that makes you piss your pants. I'm the being with a hole
in its bone forehead. I have endless skulls within skulls:
bear, fox, owl. I'm the being who was once a cuckoo,
tells no lies. I am a liar. I'm the rattlesnake that takes
the tortoise's hole. I have the face of a man who
drinks blood, of a woman of guile and deception; of an
arrogant beggar who doesn't owe you a thing.
In negative terms you cannot die for me or kill for me.
You can do nothing for me. And could I love you? I
the patient ask. Then you would not get well. No lover
gets well, and I'm not lovable. I am now within you.

I am fighting your desperation and self-loathing,
though I don't care about you. I do it for the joy of it.
I see all your identities' heads on a cyclonic body;
your faces grin or grimace, you have big stupid eyes
of old passions no one needs: desires to do good or bad,

an incapacity for reversal—everything is important,
you say; this world deserves urgent healing. *This*
is the healing. I cut off all your heads, lop, lop . . .
head after head, paste-ruby blood on the non-
dimensional floor . . . The cyclonic body's black strings.
Are you in pain, my darling? There's no pain here but
the psychic; you're afloat in a blood-sticky unuttered scream.
I'm the being who's uninterested in what people hold dear,
for I have no memory. I'm uninterested in their memorials,
their tears, and their revenge. I could never remember
to be just or fair or kind. I could never remember
to abide by the laws of science. I'm the being whose
tongue is tribes, whose forehead is the people streaming
forth from it; but I don't remember them. I don't
remember time. Yes I am your tribal deity; no
I don't reside on your planet. I have never lived. I'm
the being whose cheekbones vibrate when stars
collapse inwards. I'm the being with ears like a bat.
I hear every rumble in your small mind. I
hear the noise of your thinking; but I don't listen.
Your thoughts wouldn't bear remembering.

I'm a being who sleeps amid winds. The one
who doesn't mind death. Have I repeated myself?
Time lost its track again. Have you ever thought about
the mind of god? It isn't precisely humorless, but
it's too timeless for a story; every tale's compressed
into a dewdrop or a cell. Disordered flecks upon you.
I'm the being for whom nothing happens: now
nothing happens to you. The edges of your wound
surround a void, the torn tissue, foil-like, rustles
and shines, silver and chartreuse, the colors of a fake
nature. I encompass no nature, as no animal
thinks it's natural. I am the being that is ignorant
of your systems, tiny, and evanescent; dappling.
Your calmer, emptied body is dotted with
remnants of your thought. Your body has no
power, there is no power that matters. When
universes are created, their combustibility—explosions

in time—seem large if you are tiny. How
small are you now? Emptied you engulf all.
I am the being who smothers origin. I am
the being predating worlds, their ridiculous
assumptions: that there is matter, atmosphere, or
cerebration. Dead, you have never thought. If
you can be dead, everything is dead, or more,
uncreated, or more, was never and will never be inhabited.

The patient cries, I want to get up. No, not quite yet.
I am the being of peacefulness and stillness. I don't move.
I rise and float in your body, I make it feel like it's floating.
Isn't it, though? Where we are there's no real ground.
I inspire you to talk to the dead; I am in you, but you
and the dead are in me. I'm the being from whose mouth.
And the dead voices flow. I'm the being whose mouth
creates from dust. Whose mouth says exist again,
being nothing, being unimagined, being unreal.
I'm the being in whose mouth your senses are made,
that is, expressed. The being who has no way; the mouth
in which you see stars fall. In which your eyes live.
I'm the one who has no parent and won't accept you
as a child. I never accept your senses, I accept you
as above that dandyism. I'm the one into whose
arms you fall when you fall through all of space. The one
who tells you infinity is another hoax. I'm the being
who has no manners, or mannerisms. I have no style.
I settle on nothing; I decide nothing. This is not
a final place. There is no such place. I am the being
who whistles to you and distracts you from self-absorption.
I am the mosquito in your ear, an iridescent fly, a lightning bug.
This clearing is full of false lights, flickers that stop
when you look. I'm the being that's tricky because you
try to make me conform to your senses. You
have no senses here. You have nothing.

I have no hope then? the patient asks. There is no hope
or change. Have I not changed? the patient asks. How
could anything so empty change? Can't we go beyond

litany? the patient asks. Why bother? You are outside
time; you have never been wounded; never acted. Never
had a thought. How can I speak? Are you speaking?
This isn't happening. This is a dream, or a poem or projection.
Projected from where to where? From me to you; we aren't here.

I am the being erect like a cobra in front of you.
I would kill you if I cared to. Understand how dangerous
I am. I could make you die again; I am the being
who is the essence of repetition. I am every kind of light,
including lame light, muddy light, and flickering. I
don't have to be stronger than that. More words, more
sound, more setting: I don't have to be stronger than
that, than what there really is here. I can kill you
because you aren't real, by saying I kill you.
I can repeat it and kill you each time. I am the being
that lurks in your falseness of thought, waiting
to kill. I am the being that hears your petty tone of voice,
that snuffs out your human nature; I have no
interest in nature. I am the being who doesn't notice
good deeds. I am the being who isn't fascinated
by icicles, floods, or hurricanes. I am in everything.

I am the being that has come to you in this bad dream
to take you home. Am I special? the patient asks ironically.
I am the being who laughs like ravens. Have
you seen the raven in this clearing? Now that you
don't have the right senses. Its form stretches or
streaks across your visual field—which you don't have—
like a machine or thought you can't control.
I am the being who hasn't considered beauty. I haven't
considered humility, deity, or authority—mine or yours.
You can't name me any of your epithets: fierce,
prodigious, overarching, awe-inspiring, masterful. If
you name me one thing, you can't be healed.
To heal you must heal, now. Your phantasmagoric
wound has closed. Your thoughts have given up, finally.
I am the being within you, outside time and unhaunted.
I am the being, black night, with a moment's red

flower, unscented. I am the being who has nothing to
do with esthetics, or ideas. I am the being
that creates you, for as I am in you, you may rise.
You may ride with me back to your partial senses,
your world of claptrap and choice. Do I have to return?
the patient asks. I'm not sure I want to go back.

You will return with me soon, though this moment will last.
You will mock me because you are self-conscious. But
this healing will endure, though you are sucked
back into your details—your vicious childishness,
your sense of importance. I am the being that remains
when your world ends; I will forget it. I will forget you.
I am the being who disdains human breath as
register of process, profundity, and the real. I disdain
your mammalian communitarianism, as well as its
destructive competitiveness that gets it exactly
nowhere—for we are *now* nowhere, and this is the real.
The only place where you could be healed. But,
the patient says, if I'm healed do I really have to
be sucked in again? You may have no choice, for you
invented choice. *I* will not stay here; I will return you
and then be lost once more to your world's venal eyes.
Lost in superficial design and wings perceived as feathers;
I am the being who is anywhere, not knowing it.
You called me to heal you, will you remember you
are healed? I am the being that flashes in
a phainopepla's blackness; the being that calls
words to order and allows their meanings to sparkle.
I am the being that forgets them so I can disappear.
I am the being that disappears for pleasure. I am
the being that doesn't always call. I am the being who
has no representatives, ministers, or spouses.

I am the being that *you* are, that *you* forget. I am
the being whose horse is anxious to take you back. I
am the one within who has healed you: you stepped
outside time to find me. But you are the inventor of time
and you will go back. Can't I uninvent it? the patient asks.

You return here at night when you dream. A part
of your waking self remains; you are too dumb
to know that. And, as usual, you don't really know
what you want. Do you want the so-called love of
fellow creatures, or do you want to live in the so-called
truth? You have no words for who I am; only *I*
have those words—but you might become too petty
to find me. How did I call you this time? the patient asks.
You were sick, so sick, with your wound of thwarted longing:
you wanted the power to change the illusions you live in.
You wanted to change them to an antithetical set. You
wanted to name others wrong; you wanted to hang
words everywhere. I am the being whose words
keep dissolving; I am the being whose words aren't
sacred. I am the being whose words are mixed up
with falseness and truth as allies; I am the being
who uses words as you use the senses to handle matter.
I am the being who doesn't want to take you *home*;
I'll take you *back*. But it doesn't have to be the same as
before. If you are really healed. Even if others aren't.

I am the being connecting everything but dependent on
nothing else. You don't have to be dependent on
much else; you don't really need much. You
always define your needs too broadly. I am the being
who doesn't need, and I am in you. I am the being
composed of all knowledge, knowing nothing; the being
who doesn't want to know anything. I am the being
you are always unconscious of; you know me now
because you are unconscious; you find me asleep. Or
in your precious "special states" you think make you so
hot. Any fool who sleeps and dreams can find me. I am the
being that finds your aspirations puny. I am the being
who's unpatterned; the being who sees no patterns except
in you, for you try to identify yourself according to any
pattern you can devise, counting the cells in your eyes
or saying you are a woman or a man; you don't
have to identify yourself. And you can't. I am the being
that has no identity. I don't have to have something. I

am the being who is not praising itself and obviously
not praising you: I have been saying things in order
to heal you, because words heal. I am the only
thing that can heal you in this case. I am the being
that heals by being incontrovertible. The one who
is joyous. I am the one here, the very one. I am
the being you can't go back on; I am the being who fills
your death; the one you have no obligation to. I
am the being you, the healed, have become.

The patient says, I see my past drifting away.
The patient says: I am the being that has forgotten. It
isn't relevant to remember who I was, what my cares were.
I am the being floating above the machine I must
be part of, causing planetary death. I am sad but
I see my sorrow, dark and shapeless, with red
and orange ribbony streaks. I have to see an image
to know how I feel, because right now I don't feel.
I see. Some part of me must continue to float above.
I am the being that does not take sides in a war,
even if one side's just. I am the being that doesn't
care about justice, which creates more conflict.
I am the being that, floating, is impartial, that is,
whole. I am the being that doesn't love itself,
for that isn't necessary: I am primal. I am the
being that won't support one against another one.
I am the being whose earth transforms before my
eyes: can I only watch? That I have nothing is best
for it; I will have nothing, watching, floating.
It, the earth, primal with me, transmutes in my eyes;
but they are only eyes and don't really see.
I see with the being that floats. I am the being
that incorporates these radicalities of melting and floods,
heat and drought. I am the being that is more than
what we do to ourselves. I am the being that is larger
than the subjugation of women, that thousands-of-
years-old moment. I am the being that has never
lived on earth. I am the being whose tears are
weather. I am the being that has always been.

The patient continues: I am the being who lives in *this*
world, the world of the projections from our souls. I am a
different being from the cartoon creatures we say that
we see. I take refuge in this world that no one ever
describes. It isn't a dream. I am the being that doesn't
have to be ambitious, for I am culminative. I am the being
who has no sex and does not engender, for everything's
born. I am the being that isn't having a vision. I am
the being who is omnipresent, because I am receptive to
anyone else's mind—anyone's projection—wherever they are.
I am the being that doesn't worship, pray, or cower.
I am the being that isn't a believer. Isn't humble. I'm ready now.

Blinding the white horse in front of me. I will ride
light back. I have healed myself in light and will
return, in light, to light. Yes, an image. I am an image
now, again, born in the eyes of others. I am the being
that is born wrongly in human eyes. I had always
seen and named myself as I was told to. Who has
seen me? But forget that, riding the white rayed
horse through greenish-white air towards home. I am
the being that flows through space, but there is no
space, only being. The stars, shapeless pendants,
brilliantly conform to no pattern, against the
fabric around me, the only silk I can see.
It isn't dark? Are you with me? I speak to any patient,
in the battle against the illness of living as we do—
the horizon our healing wound, seen by our noncellular
eyes, our eyes new images. You are light and your
fingertips are petals, mirrors silver and gold. I'm the being
unqualified by pronouns; I am the being that was always
frightened by my inclusion of you as my weakness.
We see each other now as the one image, light—
there is no light. Riding towards you as light,
emitting it, I am the being that creates the sun.

PRIVATE LIFE: THE NAMES

□

She rose up and told me   what to do al-   most in the rags of chance.
My name isn't Chance it's   Then the night hides   her name for we're moving
Those words won't let me trap   them in your gram-   mar: they've got their
     own rule

So will you approach, as love, knowing all this will dissolve futurely
into bits of us bright. As we enter the real reality
after this breaks up and before that I'd
          heal
          you

Fate started here. The sha-   ttered for you be-   gan to believe bodies

I was sent, slowly to   know who I am—   my life is dangerous
You will receive in flashes   a new knowledge   in language you won't know.

Will you spy for us who beauty wings of death. Whose side am I on?
The dead as Against the living. We've been asking you to all along
since you. What am I reporting on? "Everything is a report . . ."

                                             Am a spy or prophet?
Both. Learn to speak levels at once. And in the heart of the light burst
we acquired speech in a dream so fascinated I couldn't stop.
The dead people want to know why everything turned out this way.
Because I am there in   the dream, and it   happens. As true as history
So if you want that I'm   a Cassandra   I'm like that.

                                      Reporting to the dead
                                 I don't know why it was
a tragedy, the world.   I don't know our   language anymore, man
Expectation's a drag.   What did you ex-   pect? That the failure grows

Became spy. Gradually hooked on it and then am its details
there's no way out working for man from the dead recruited I sit at
table talking and then more of world during. I refuse to submit
yet I am reporting to this dead young jerk. Their representative
No you're really reporting to us, say all the dead. We've fingered you
Why should *I* know why the world failed? You were born so you'd know.

What are you telling me? THESE THOUGHTS

And when lightning covered
in sheets the surround see it
but there was no rain a drop
                that I think
to you. And you think back its
damp odor

in the telepathy of dreams
TALK TO ME

YOU HAVE TO READ MY THOUGHT

I keep that next to me always
I know the dead flashing thought to
each other. The thought structured
a form with shifting edges. You
must learn *it* what about the vocal?
the form is that same sheet lightning

but we hear the poetry.

To ex-   press the first twist   of
that which isn't good for you: Fate

Help me emit this de-   scription: I   saw her get up to be.
She stole me like she did   others, but she   invented herself for
me: my unhappiness.   She is person-   al, I'm prepersonal.

   I was sup-   flash posed
   to be in character al-   flash ready
   Never   But. you see
   did   ALREADY I remember death
I was slowly beginning to
I was slowly begin-   ning to: slow down   but I was talking to
them.

She wanted a body, called BODY. (But I
didn't)
And she takes it from the   chaos and she   puts it: while I'm just talking. She
makes this stupid stuff bod-   y, boded, while   Look, this is what happened!

What do you see?
We have one sense not precisely the mind
what we see is it presently, different one of us is god and the other is too.
Individually? We are each that. The air is sweet. Time? Not a predicament.
You (we) were given enormous (you—we—took) degree of differentiation; but we
screwed up.
Right away, didn't we? How did we manage to find, or invent, Fate?
Something about . . .
And why was I (so) fated?
You have transcended it how by riding (it)

      lines draw a house or a person
      inventing you.

You are fate, Spy.

The dead are working on   the universe: they're in its shifting walls.
My father's mother, whom   I never met,   says, I'm here for you lit-
tle girl. My tragic aunt   is there, she weeps.   I ask her how she is
I'm okay. I ask my fa-   ther, How long does   anguish last? But it's not
like living, time isn't   the same. The dead   poets are working on
their poems. The dead are   working on the   universe. The moment is
itself, has its own, we're in.   But that's the dead.   Why did life turn out *like*?

Fate says, I needed near-   ly to destroy   you in order to choose you
you the shatterproof   one and now you're ready.   What are you? I
ask. Not a person, I'm   almost tempor-   al; but I compress time.

Is Dorothy still tra-   gic? I ask the   dead, or is she just crying?
They say, That must be part   of what we're ask-   ing. I did it, he says.
No you didn't, I say.   She shudders a-   gainst him. I need to know.
We both need to know why.

Is she working on the u-   niverse now? Yes   of which all you see is
your dress.

You don't want to
                    meet her on what level
of parking spiral.
        James is here James's ring

Are you afraid of me   behind the cars

    Once, no one was afraid. Because
they knew they were already dead.
    Who is James? any
    calls up. Meet me at a table with your
data.
    They're in traffic without caring, that
is my report.

        By the river. we'll go down by.
        So we went down there and shone a flashlight on the bank.
        Fate a tiny woman hatching from a circle in the mud. The size of a baby frog.
        Why tell this   you want to know what happens   The rains come precisely
        to wash her away but she holds on
        to a tule. There are no more tules.
        Why did this happen?
        This is the other thing I the spy saw: I see that when I die
        the kind of world we know
        rolls up into a circular cell and is gone. The new arises, and I am not afraid.
        Thank you for your intelligence.

    if it has only been a million years or more that there have been people a flash in
the pan where was I before that? well you were dead.

        eye   sewer   come out of sewer seeing
        spying

        for the reader   (the beautiful dead.)

tell me the truth
IN OUR INSTANT

The moment
is itself.

The real question, how does it work?
since I saw that,
rolls up into a circular cell and is gone. at one's death
that is I *saw* that this reality simply
disappears   not precisely fake but
disposable—a disposable *version*. It's evident
that we create our portion of it
with our senses: what we see is for them, or
by them . . . It's one system. So
when there's not that one, what *is* there? or
what *is* there?

The dead say, Nothing is precluded. It is a partial vision . . .
it goes away and you   almost forget   it but emotions stay
I feel, Dad said, that I   did wrong. Here
there is no *doing*,

NOT PROPER FLASH

listen   Can you hear my
I need you   tremendous impact   deeds indissoluble.
          Something clinging
          we work on it.

I   far
am debriefed   from
           epiphany   the which I had
if the emotional   tone clings in death
short tragic Greeks with eyes
           and I will sacrifice   here, remember
As I sacrificed my   self as girl. for   you. though I never be-
lieved in her keep me warm

   Are you getting this cog-   nitive page a   only itself flashes
I, and he's waiting, dead   Who sacrificed   me? her eyes she cries with
blue and a voice
   Longevity is not   very long, I   say to her. like a fool

Still in the novel? I   just want to be   where you are. Who   even
if unhap
a string of thinkings, of   instant transmis-
   But what of the debrief-
ing:
they put her on the al-   tar, they thought there   was a god but there was
just us the immortals   in a sense of   what else can there be? not
another a shitty   dictator in   the sky. instead you're there
and I'm everywhere—   scattered and wise   from my pain: what do you
know?
What I say. not simple.

124

When you're dead the moment   is itself. May-   be that can be lived, live
one domed enclosure in   which one's selfhood   perceives but cedes its
importance. It was a   musical e-   vent as I took part in
it, a poetry read-   ing that became   a concert. The reader,
an infant, has a speech   impediment.   You don't have to know what
he's saying if you're there.   That's one part of   my story for I can't
stay in that all-moment . . .

need to kill me maybe   everything's going wrong:

"Don't wear the crown of thorns to meet
me." It doesn't come off. goes with Fate
above the eyebrows where I'm too intelligent . . .
You have to make it even more interesting
                              evil. To be that always a
simply self-assertion, disbelief, and put-down

Chose to be in time—who?
                              it left the hole
     which is not that, is it?
Written on the sky scribbled by lightning
   Alice Exist   and in the language of
the future. But now it   was known, both the   language and the future.
Don't you dead know? it's   already hap-   pened but we know it scram-
bled, heaped, chaosed. Though know   that it has failed   by the time I: all those
CARS.
          scram I FLASH bled. on the altar

I've been going through all   the drawers and   cabinets. Can't find it.
While they're away; they don't   know anything   anyway . . .

Money and what you do   for it. How to   stay inside the machine
you were born to. Product   of people's im-   agination, our hu-
man room? They are too stu-   pid to invent   any thing but an ap-
pliance

      When Fate arrives
      What's in the cabinet

He stands in front saying   do I have to   have an erection to   open it?
As if *I* have the key.   I don't work here,   I say.

A NEW QUOTE BRAIN

I've spied on him and determined there's
nothing in his   head   but linear FITS

BUT we've CARBON dated it,   *linear* works!

      Oh   There are several kinds
of time going on at   the same time. That   of the line, that of the
dead, and that of the leap.   Curved and sudden.   You now know expertly . . .
though it may not be worth   knowing: how to   flay someone until they
sing out TRAGIC LIES the   leap from the a-   moeba to me has hap-

pened in an instant, man   though you're still queued   with the erection; and
we're both dead at the same time.

BLACK VIOLETS

Whatever happened was first dreamed
so you'd know it was going to   we first spoke
in a dream and then spoke. Who dreamed it?
I was in charge of that dream. But
first it was dreamed that I would dream it.
However you name it that wasn't the way
it was. Black violets, we beauty acquired
I'm on an altar in a dream. Anyone's dis-
posable except for the king.

I AM A MULTIPLE AGENT,

                              and it's
driving me A nervous wreck if I talk about
Dorothy or cars. Cars are our home. Dorothy Dad
signed the papers for, under medical advice
they always so much smarter than us
No one's sure how she died   after the lobotomy
in her early 20s
                    I assure you I did not want to leave
She knew in her violence something violent
would happen   to her.
Chaos was calmer I go there whenever I can
it doesn't *try*. That's what it's *about*.

I don't want this part where   I don't know if   I've dreamed it or not. Cars
everywhere and no air   in the air. I   foresaw but didn't dream
But what I didn't dream   first was being   talked to by the dead. I
or did I; but I did–   n't think you were   *real*. I need to talk to
you, Daddy said. I thought,   I could have stayed   out of this one; I didn't.
Deeper and deeper. No   more lyric po-   ems or love affairs. A
provision lurks, O where   is beauty? You   still haven't told me what
happened to the world. I   do know but don't   yet know how to say it.

Dorothy tell me some-   thing. I only   remember that it all hurt.
I wanted to be a   singer, I think.   Then I was taken, it
took me. That was possi-   ble. There's too much   possibility. Fate
Fate distributes it to   me. And me, I   say. A wind in my head.

You're not interested enough in us one says
Of course I am I say lying You don't listen
when I tell you about the car I
think the car's a beauty I say is this an in-
terrogation And the other one says We need
to make sure you're with us a human a
person you know Who else would I be We
think you're with the other party / the other
country / a whole other room And what a-
bout the dead she says I thought you were
a feminist why don't you agree with us
about names a public woman and the other
one says though you seem so emotional you
have no feeling
                    I hope not I say I'm working
for myself Just like that Yes I lie and I lie How
could I work for the dead (You must under-
stand I learned to lie in the last
elect- and also in the car park where James's
where he wanted to ring me but I didn't
have a phone.) And you don't have a cell
phone she says
                    This is all imaginary, isn't
it a voice of a dead man says. Yes and no
I've been lying to everyone for several years
because it's easier I don't care about any-
thing they care And I don't go anywhere
What can they do to you? he says Not
communicate with Not give work to Or
credence to Excommunication's economic
death. Which he says is death. Maybe not
Wouldn't they all still love you No I say
I'm a liar. Is this true. No but when I
tell the truth, but then it can be a joke
that I talk to the dead An Imagination or
Just another useless poem who cares about
that not even other poets they don't read
them they just talk about them. How can

you be a poet and talk to me he says I don't
know but you wouldn't have invested so much
in me if I weren't. Did you always know he
says that you were like this I've always lied
I do work for myself. And us they all say the dead Yes.

An experiment?
Always had
        my ID at
the beginning   (my secret ID) (without my name?)
      At the beginning the   existence of   myriad IDs be–   came
      Why Why not if the fut–   ure was known? (was   always going to be)

But you were born in 1945!
                         My identity
was quasi-
dormant but
existent be–
fore?

PLAY TO THE SHADOW
OF BEAUTY

        until it is a planet. I am a
plant.
    I was always but didn't have to until

        Point
being to try out this specificity. We couldn't handle it. We

were not that smart: diffuse   intelligence   narrowed as we were boxed
in by our flesh and sen–   ses. These attri–   butes and that of dying.
You die from the exper–   iment back in–   to the vast conglom-
erate of all the I   Ds. *of* ID;   of forgotten being.

Who planted you here? Oh   that. In a flash.   Maybe I planted myself.

She starts to get used to   being sacrificed   in time. Counting, it's a-
bout.
You want it, Achilles   says. But he will   die too. Cassandra wants
to too. Get out of time.   Iphigeni-   a's led there, leaders lead
us, I didn't want to,   Dorothy says.   My dad starts to cry, he
hates losing his sister. But   you're together   now! I keep going over
it. That's what I do when   I don't contact   you for a long—well, *time,*
he says.

      The pain bursts she says
      then goes away again.

And if you had lived and   sung, married had   kids? Would still be here, she
says. What is it for? I, Iph-   igenia   says, am I and know from
you too. But what did we   need to know? Ev-   erything is what I
know, a headache
a planet . . . of worms. they'll   die out; it's vast-   er here, he says. Help us,
though. Our thoughts spread across   the universe—   need to make them better—

They put her down they place her, Calchas slits her throat he's disgusting and it's athels
the cemetery hot and grey after each of you. An experiment every step is one while the
priests economists and rich men   try to hang on to   values. The only valuable is?
What you know, he says, in a poem. And my love. Which is visible here in death I emit it
it's part of what you're left with when you die. I haven't loved enough I think.

The sacrifice blood spills everywhere even in the safe house—she gave in
to the gods but they didn't exist the blood did. Tragic lies in the drawer blood
in the lower drawer and in the lowest one sym-

Since I say we are symbols   for what we act-   ually are that we
don't know, I might as well   say anything,   standing in for myself.

You know, my father says   that I a dead   man talk to you.

But you

don't know a lot of words, I say.
It's not words, he says.   It's a cash   commitment . . .
What does that mean?
I trust you.
These words are standing in for, I say, what you say.

In the safe house a man   might bother you.   The agency's files are
a mess. My agents are,   you know, reason,   reflection, the senses . . .
That is, I'm not them. I'm   something else, Yes,   he says, you're in essence
like us. A soul. We need   your agents to   report to you. Oh great.
I myself am nothing . . .   You are you I   love you he says. How do
you know that I say be-   cause as an ab-   solute there's the exact.
You didn't say that Yes   I did. Doroth-   y says, But there's this mud.
Junk he says, can't get rid.   Gotcha, I say.

Fragility is a condition being in time I didn't choose it . . . The black violets so
crushable. And your ideas that I don't need but you hold on to in standing-in words.
I'm tempted to say what happened was to women.

He says your mainstay cloak.

Cloaking what?

A further horror.

This is my secret I   D that was al-   ways alive. What it I
Ds—I. I. When I lo-   cate I I turn   into wavelengths feel them.
Shimmering, vibrant, a-   hum. What do I   do while I continue?

inform. I'm the offi-   cial informant.

We came here vibrating singing myths
we didn't come here that's a story
we came to be. I didn't
you need to know that our   interpreta-   tion of the past can't be
right. Time is clumpy, clustered;   one day the cli-   mate breaks soon. Does that
happen? I think so—is   it a story   or some language? I . . . it's
already . . .

How fixed?

Were you by chance? Once the   identity's assumed it was never
changed. The planet had no   other future,   or destiny? its end
death. What happens? happened—   and some saw, all   would have died of course in
any case: IDs don't die?   So many more   IDs than there once were—

But, he says, what happened? What happened to Dorothy?

You sang with Gabriel Payne's band.
When I was only sixteen.
Country western and popular? I heard that you met Tex Ritter.
We are all musical aren't we Albert   I think our selves sing
do you hear it? when I don't
shudder and change it
I was real pretty but then I got called to be too different—I attacked her.
   Momma.

Like a dream, but you do it they
took me, later, to the mental ward, to change me.
Is there always a further horror?
On earth
Can a word   say it
She bowed her head first and is buried near the others, plain cross.

Am I like her because   I talk to you?   Crows above me mocking
black arcs Who are you re-   porting to, the   young dead James? it wouldn't
matter if they called you   crazy, they are   ignorant men he now
says. Dorothy were you   mentally ill?   I was too angry but
they were worse, they cut a   piece out of my   brain, it was worse than rape

---

Who is this intel for?   Dad feels so sick.   But he's dead. I get an
especial sensiti-   vity from him   and Dorothy. They sing
When you go *back* to the   dead—after you've   died—transformed by talent,
horror. If you're a jerk   you're a stunted   dead person . . . can you change
in death? I don't know yet   James says. I gather   up your intelligence
but I don't know what to   do with it. I   don't know how to be . . . an-
ything but empty.

If you can define your   own cruelty,   you can go there. Where? the
earth . . . I think. No the death   I mean *be* there.   Understand who you were,
But is it *real* enough

                    now? Nothing's real   for me, James says. He's
thus asking, but
cruelty's not mine . . .
I . . .   a possibility,
     So you kill something or flash see

                              I saw it was on earth. But you,
Daddy, never did that.
          What happened? he says again,

                                   Fate, I say,
has claws. Dorothy you   were cruel . . .

                         I thought she was *hurting* me:
making me *her* will. But
          why all this? he

               asks.
                         I say, Fate isn't a pro-
gram, as much as a pounce. A-   live I know a-   bout it and shake from know-
ing, fearful because my kind   is cruel and   aren't I of that kind?
Just knowing this once gave   me a breakdown.   I called it my flashes
Flash you see you have the   capacity   to kill.

                              I shot small game
to eat, he says. I don't like for us
to be divided in-   to categor-   ies of prey. Call it love
that I need to eat you?   That's no good, it's   still fated, fearful

But love is too. FLASH FLASH

                    The jerk says I   don't understand . . . this . . .

Wish the railroad didn't   run so near—that   linearity, just
to *run off.* When you're dead   you can't . . . Maybe   you don't want to? disap-
pear. Dorothy wanted to sing . . .

When I woke up after the
operation. I just stared then,
I didn't *know*   but you *know*
now; I can't get over that they
did it   to *me.* It's like *I* did
it, he says. You   didn't oper-
ate. And you visited and brought
money, as if that would make
me better, because that was
what we hadn't had . . .

SAY in a flash:
something I can't forgive . . . Can't die right.

WHY DID I HAVE TO GO THROUGH IT

Is
the universe trying to learn how to be MORAL?
as the big mind it is . . .

I Alice acting out for this *gigantic* jerk I'm part of—
this makes me shi-   ver, frightful death,
science is too *stupid*   to go there, I   say. You have to find it
all out from me; as *my*   informants bleed.   Dog my brain, tell me *shit.*

Then the gangsters
broke all the bottles in the drugstore
and stuck the glass   in their flesh . . .

We don't *know*
the rules, never did

The gangsters won't be healed.

It was invented all at once in the cell but had to play out in time. Was it completely predict-
able or -ed? ForeTOLD. You could see it spin out of the cell—a room I guess of the uni-
verse—and unwind. Okay first the "invented" part. *Who?* Did it? It's as if it just happened
to get predicted. Still no reason. I'm so sticky with Fate I can hardly move for fear of it.
Maybe the point *is* that you can always   see or feel it   coming. The beginning
and the unraveling   at the same time, you see. You need to get slightly ahead.

The black petals brush my   shoulders; she al-   ways knew she would be sac-
rificial and either   fought against it   violently pre-
cipitating the de-   struction, or she   succumbed, deer who can't run
frozen-legged the purple   beggar cannot   open her mouth and scream
what would not affect the   righteous men.   No language but their own.

You're killing me because you think you owe more to the men like you than to any
woman—owe that which the gods want. Prove the gods exist, Agamemnon.

I'm trying to get to   a simple e-   nough place so it's clear to
you. My thought to yours. These   words themselves are   telepathic and you
get the whole damn thought, its   field, if you get   it.

WAIT candelabra in   the tree shadows,   sometimes if you SEE it's
PAIN. How much anguish can   you tolerate?   I don't understand why
you're so unhappy. I   don't either, it's   in my head. But I feel
it when I see, I see   in it. Of it.   Dark the parks, even in
day.

Why did you feel like that   I could again   Can you feel like that when
you're dead? Not as bad, Dot   says. But there's a   pain in lack of reasons.
We are still reasona-   ble, he says. I   am serving two masters,
I say, you and the liv-   ing. It could be-   come painful, confusing.

I can't really tell anyone I talk to you,
that is part of our strangeness; nor is
this an allowed story, my spymasters. The
poetry of it's jagged, plain-talking, hurtful—
I should be writing an Iliad instead. You're
writing for us, he says. It should still be
beautiful. Why? he says. Not that it isn't . . .
The perception of beauty comforts . . . the
universe, I say. Which perceives itself.
How do we know that? he says. I
just know; I am it.

What are you doing right   now I ask him   I'm watching everything
it roars; it singing lights   up. I'm not un-   happy just puzzled and
talking strings of it like   you. Translated
          SEE what you think
          he pets it as if
          but the energy form
          disap-

When I call my soul upfront, I say,
I can locate it . . . the Survivor—
what more will she let go of?
The rings . . . And the Terror? That
made you what you are.
Does Achilles feel it?   He's afraid he   has nothing but his fame
something for every-   one else but him.   It's empty. Can mine not
be? Oh I see through it   already.

We were ALways in this   other time. That   you find your way into
And then I AM, says A-   chilles, I am   that. But I, I say, am
THAT, TOO. NOW in this sa-   cred time. I am   sacred, infinite, but
named MY name . . .

    covered with jagged beauty facets . . .
you would make them be parti-   cles in anoth-   er more finite world that's
ours.

Leave your tame lines, your spilled   blood in the safe   house, to enter re al-
ity with ME.
         Why aren't
                you too large for
   this investigation?

The jagged pieces of   your dress lap as   waves on the onyx strand . . .
They have planted me here,   named. To speak as,   as I get closer, they.
The cutout jerk or James   says, You've stopped   being a credible
live human though. Are you   ready to de-   fect back? I have no de-
fects now, I'm free. I'm act-   ing out of love,   I'm the freest savior
ever known!

The idea of evil here is   brought by US to   death, because we can call
it out ONLY by liv-   ing. Fate made us   call it: the bigger mind
us made ONE call it. The   so-called uni-   verse. It wants to know why
its powers are destruct-   ive. It would like   to change. From birth on out.

Likes this time of morning   when the light fin-   ally comes as night's pain
resolving into first   dawn. "I used to   think it was *my* feeling
but now I think it's its."   Then waking I   am in mental hurt that
gradually dissolves . . .   it is uncon-   nected to anything:
it is its, the uni-   verse's. *It* has   it, I am *it*, the both.

Oh I am afraid of being so duplicit . . . while everyone works,
thinking they are safe.
                    My apartment's
unsafe, for everything I am is my mind, that never leaves me. (Almost to speak
as if I weren't it?) Everything reaching to be present, telling me what it is or
that it is: all of danger. (BUT the dead are all right!) But I myself, it the universe says,
am dangerous.

Why are you/we violent?

I don't know how to act—create—without massive disruption.

Why haven't you stayed in chaotic, initial form?

It's possible I mostly have but you can't locate that.

"Evil pushes out evil"
yes I'm aware of that.   The world's motto   doesn't know it, does it
if power turns out, no   *is* bad, can I   be good and also save
you? who? I'm unclear. James: I'm only told   that you *will* . . . save. He says,
we are bonded. In ser-   vice. To no power—   evil pushes out e-
vil: thus we'd be create-   d. I'm not a   creature. Invisible,

my me-ness has no interest in itself but is itself. I

WHA HAP

What's the advantage of creation   over uncreation?
Ad-vantage, James says. Of life now over life before
everything was a report, cruelly spoken.
You are finding yourself out. But I was always a spy for you,
so I could do both.

———————————————————————

Walked where the black waves beat   the strand. Before   becoming violets and
sand.

———————————————————————

I guess, Daddy says, Death is getting remade too . . .

I'M SENDING YOU ALL YOUR FLASHES
I CAN'T FIND BEAUTY
YOU'RE STILL IN THE OLD SYSTEM, JUST LOOK!

Do you know how to think without articulating? I ask a dead man.
There's another kind of articulation, he says.

———————————————————————

have you called me to all my dreams

the problem is that the earth is a killing room: that's what happened
why? they say. It isn't boring here in death
Then why was life invented

The words being pulled apart into puls-
ating syllables   Others driving me mad
trying to be dinky shamans. Not them and
not your contemporaries
we take all the best like you For what? I
scream. This. I just wanted to write some
great poems Oh it's all so much *larger*
Poetry is so much *larger*. What happened to
the couched blonde dead friend of what
is James for no points? There will no
longer be any points. The universe is
changing not like matter provisionally
staked out but, according to its temper.
I am Cassandra now unbelieved but a
prediction might be lovely O my little spies
and cutouts. Trying to be better the blonde
says. You are? Stuck with these provisional
looks of my century species, which I no
longer believe in. Do you have a name too?
I guess it's Jamie, Cassandra. How I say can
we make them listen? Wear you know
like the clothes of when the Wall fell. Between
                              We have taken
you. because—
but *you* have to figure it out,
Better. I say I don't know how
to make them accept me. I thought she
says you were a better spy than that
I am duplicitous but I can't pander.
I can't just write how they—oh various
different who's—like it.
And I have to tell my father, who is not
Priam, what happened. Should you con-
centrate on that she says? The dead are
hard to get through to harder than
beauty. Or excitement. But you have
these pages—which I love, and you are dead
but am I really talking to you? Some-

times my father *really* talks to me
but sometimes I'm not sure. Out of this
greyness I write to live humans, too. *They*
need to know this part. If they can
find the grey they can gradually talk to the dead.

THE STORY

I am the story leading you to freedom all one and element
There would be no need if pieces of lake or light hadn't broken off
Plain or what became dumped space orchid bent filled with us litter
I yet being all and stood there beginning destined to lead you
If the god's winds overturned the ships of me they were still lies
There's no dying where I'm leading you is that realization
Thus all your needs are vain you hysterics it takes little to
Feed and house you you see through a millions-of-years smeared
Lens you have no enemies we're from the same and only
Frequencies a visible spectrum including prophecy
Remember seeing it that you'd be born later forgetting
We are what we saw the ones walking fragilely but we aren't fragile
I'm leading you to strength a lake on a hill of insolent pleasures
Blue or green lake red lake I'm leading you to humor your own joke
All of matter has humor planets and galaxies laugh at their
Piecemeal forms their having fallen apart not fallen like angels
But being displaced from their unity their first one as I am laugh
It's not funny that we murder each other we can laugh at it sorrowfully
A convulsion like that's how we became when all exploded all that re-
Vulsion or any language you want we know who we are
In a one first language we've forgotten but ignorantly use
I'm leading you to the lake of un-ignorance on the hill of
Un-folly somewhere you know but never quite remember lovers
Taking it easily not earning money nor buying too much
The place of purple lake and orange calvary I have been there
Have suffered and shaken to lead you through a membrane door towards trans-
Figuration how might you be figured after your complex death
You have never needed objects or this queasiness of products
Your definitions of living kill you into a frenetic boredom
I am leading you I who don't play with you at your trivial ambitions
To a lake colored by memory spreading and deepening
Remember when we first stood here calling to each other where
Have we been or will be but we are what is knowing us as semblants
As souls as the one mind a dovecote *a* persons *a* languages
Without any deity but us without any need but to know
Each other's minds again after our presumed deaths reunited
One by one as slowly as we've been alone calmly remember

Why there was matter in the first place why we were there at that shore
Of the lake of space colored with every lake calling spirits I
Have led you back or forward lovers memory is everywhere
The universe being memory trembling our minds creating it grand
Were we never shattered then and what we think we see merest iconography
I remember when the doves were let out grey oh my figures
How have we made us by a liberation in sleep of potency
The air was still at first and we the dead already there want to
Remember hearts voices and a light-mind sourceless us do you remember

I remember the random absolute I'm leading you to
The only thing there is we can't conceive of such explicitness
Entered upon with the foresight of what are we seeing with
Our and it didn't have to be eyes integral seeing
I'm leading you to before I remember the dark desert high-
Way lead you on from the first shabby town where we nonetheless loved
Each other why not tacky lovers a judgment from the later
Self-conscious one I will be leading you to the mountain no imped-
Iment but your friend to slip through the folds of gigantic
Parental I remember immediately that we have memories we
Allow ourselves them I know you're my lovers but what else is there
Others led you to doom I lead you to the casting away of possessions
Like doom like fate like familial indebtedness to a past
One always saw coming and can see as far as you can think
I remember we destroyed things haplessly I'm standing with
You in your deaths you know how you became enmeshed in a game
Of material invention seeing only the bodies you agreed
To see I lead you from that pettiness back to the original past
Into the original future you are beginning to descry
She went there and saw it language and memory pliant
Self at any time how did we make the universe
We pressed on our memories before we had them
I remember going through it saying ah ha ha ha or something so
Obviously who we are even the mountains walking to
And through the eras before I was born do you understand
I to you and now is tiny a part of overarching death
Name of our existence to which I'm leading you the dead talk to us
Saying we need your help for our being is endless we're in this together
We're creating ourselves out of thought and speech I am leading you

To porousness I am destroying politics I remember walk-
Ing on my street thinking I have achieved freedom who else has
It's a state of nonpossession for the universe we are
Possesses itself always releasing itself simultaneously
Through a door of self going on in temporal expansion
It is a miracle she said in the sense that there's no explanation
The miracle lies across the bottom where words support us
And are us my children cry out with me turn on the lights

Alice Notley was born in Bisbee, Arizona, on November 8, 1945, and grew up in Needles, California. She was educated at Barnard College and at the Writers' Workshop, University of Iowa. During the late sixties and early seventies she lived a peripatetic, rather outlawish poet's life (San Francisco, Bolinas, London, Essex, Chicago) before settling on New York's Lower East Side. For sixteen years there, she was an important force in the eclectic second generation of the so-called New York School of poetry. She has never tried to be anything but a poet, and all her ancillary activities have been directed to that end. Notley is the author of more than forty books of poetry. Her book-length poem *The Descent of Alette* was published by Penguin in 1996, followed by *Mysteries of Small Houses* (1998), which was one of three finalists for the Pulitzer Prize and was the winner of the *Los Angeles Times* Book Award for Poetry. More recent publications include *Grave of Light: Selected Poems 1970–2005*, for which she won the Academy of American Poets' Lenore Marshall Poetry Prize; *In the Pines*, which inspired an album of music by the indie duo AroarA; *Culture of One*, a verse novel set in a small desert town; *Negativity's Kiss*, a detective novel in verse; and the epic *Benediction*. Notley has also received the Griffin Poetry Prize (for her 2001 collection *Disobedience*), the Shelley Memorial Award from the Poetry Society of America, and an Academy Award in Literature from the American Academy of Arts and Letters. In 2015 she was awarded the Poetry Foundation's Ruth Lilly Poetry Prize, which recognizes the outstanding lifetime achievement of a living U.S. poet. She lives and works in Paris.

PENGUIN POETS

JOHN ASHBERY
Selected Poems
Self-Portrait in a Convex
    Mirror

PAUL BEATTY
Joker, Joker, Deuce

JOSHUA BENNETT
The Sobbing School

TED BERRIGAN
The Sonnets

LAUREN BERRY
The Lifting Dress

PHILIP BOOTH
Lifelines: Selected Poems
    1950–1999

JULIANNE BUCHSBAUM
The Apothecary's Heir

JIM CARROLL
Fear of Dreaming:
    The Selected Poems
Living at the Movies
Void of Course

ALISON HAWTHORNE DEMING
Genius Loci
Rope
Stairway to Heaven

CARL DENNIS
Another Reason
Callings
New and Selected Poems
    1974–2004
Practical Gods
Ranking the Wishes
Unknown Friends

DIANE DI PRIMA
Loba

STUART DISCHELL
Dig Safe

STEPHEN DOBYNS
Velocities: New and Selected
    Poems: 1966–1992

EDWARD DORN
Way More West

ROGER FANNING
The Middle Ages

ADAM FOULDS
The Broken Word

CARRIE FOUNTAIN
Burn Lake
Instant Winner

AMY GERSTLER
Crown of Weeds
Dearest Creature
Ghost Girl
Medicine
Nerve Storm
Scattered at Sea

EUGENE GLORIA
Drivers at the Short-Time Motel
Hoodlum Birds
My Favorite Warlord

DEBORA GREGER
By Herself
Desert Fathers, Uranium Daughters
God
Men, Women, and Ghosts
Western Art

TERRANCE HAYES
Hip Logic
How to Be Drawn
Lighthead
Wind in a Box

NATHAN HOKS
The Narrow Circle

ROBERT HUNTER
Sentinel and Other Poems

MARY KARR
Viper Rum

JACK KEROUAC
Book of Blues
Book of Haikus
Book of Sketches

JOANNA KLINK
Circadian
Excerpts from a Secret Prophecy
Raptus

JOANNE KYGER
As Ever: Selected Poems

ANN LAUTERBACH
Hum
If in Time: Selected Poems,
    1975–2000
On a Stair
Or to Begin Again
Under the Sign

CORINNE LEE
Plenty

PHILLIS LEVIN
May Day
Mercury
Mr. Memory & Other Poems

PATRICIA LOCKWOOD
Motherland Fatherland
    Homelandsexuals

WILLIAM LOGAN
Macbeth in Venice
Madame X
Strange Flesh
The Whispering Gallery

ADRIAN MATEJKA
The Big Smoke
Mixology

MICHAEL MCCLURE
Huge Dreams: San Francisco
    and Beat Poems

ROSE MCLARNEY
Its Day Being Gone

DAVID MELTZER
David's Copy: The Selected
    Poems of David Meltzer

ROBERT MORGAN
Dark Energy
Terroir

CAROL MUSKE-DUKES
An Octave above Thunder
Red Trousseau
Twin Cities

ALICE NOTLEY
Certain Magical Acts
Culture of One
The Descent of Alette
Disobedience
In the Pines
Mysteries of Small Houses

WILLIE PERDOMO
The Essential Hits of Shorty
    Bon Bon

LIA PURPURA
It Shouldn't Have Been Beautiful

LAWRENCE RAAB
The History of Forgetting
Visible Signs: New and Selected
    Poems

BARBARA RAS
The Last Skin
One Hidden Stuff

MICHAEL ROBBINS
Alien vs. Predator
The Second Sex

PATTIANN ROGERS
Generations
Holy Heathen Rhapsody
Wayfare

ROBYN SCHIFF
A Woman of Property

WILLIAM STOBB
Absentia
Nervous Systems

TRYFON TOLIDES
An Almost Pure Empty Walking

SARAH VAP
Viability

ANNE WALDMAN
Gossamurmur
Kill or Cure
Manatee/Humanity
Structure of the World
    Compared to a Bubble

JAMES WELCH
Riding the Earthboy 40

PHILIP WHALEN
Overtime: Selected Poems

ROBERT WRIGLEY
Anatomy of Melancholy and
    Other Poems
Beautiful Country
Earthly Meditations: New and
    Selected Poems
Lives of the Animals
Reign of Snakes

MARK YAKICH
The Importance of Peeling
    Potatoes in Ukraine
Unrelated Individuals Forming a
    Group Waiting to Cross